THE ULTIMA

EXCELLENT BOOKS

EXCELLENT BOOKS
94 BRADFORD ROAD
WAKEFIELD
WEST YORKSHIRE WF1 2AE
TEL / FAX: (01924) 315147

Printed 1997
Reprinted 1998
Reprinted 2000

ISBN 1 901464 02 4

Front cover photo: Climbing out of Garrigill towards Nenthead
Rear cover photo: Looking back from the Old Coach Road towards St. Johns in the Vale

Printed in Great Britain by
Carnmoor Print and Design
95-97 London Road
Preston
Lancashire
PR1 4BA

CONTENTS

Near Lydgetts Junction on the Consett to Sunderland Railway Path

INTRODUCTION

WHAT IS THE C2C ?

The C2C can fairly claim to be the most popular and most widely known long distance cycle route in the UK, completed by many thousands of people each year. It is to cycling what the Pennine Way is to walking. The longest option runs for around 140 miles across the northern edge of the Lake District, across the Eden Valley and across the beautifully bleak Northern Pennines before dropping down to the post-industrial landscape of the North-East. There are optional starting points (Whitehaven or Workington) and a choice of end point (Tynemouth or Sunderland).

The route uses a mix of specially constructed cycle paths, off-road tracks and minor roads, only occasionally straying onto short sections of main road where necessary. Waymarked for much of the way (although signs are sometimes removed by souvenir hunters) it can be completed by the whole gamut of cyclists, whilst not being designed for any specific sub-group of the cycling world, such as mountain-bikers or tourers. Although undoubtedly a challenge, containing several serious climbs, it is completed by those with little experience of cycling and committed bikers alike. Careful choice of alternative sections should allow just about any type of bike to complete the route (tricycles may have difficulty passing through barriers and on some climbs). However, having at least 18 gears will be a godsend and avoid a lot of uphill pushing.

Why so popular? The C2C was the brainchild of cycling charity Sustrans (see pg 5) who have promoted it as their 'flagship' long-distance route and it has undoubtedly tapped a demand for long-distance cycle holidays. This desire to escape the traffic on two wheels is surely a reaction against the road congestion that has become one the great logistical and health problems of our age. Many previous non-cyclists have successfully attempted this challenging route and have become more regular cyclists. Another vital area of Sustrans work, alongside its promotion of recreational routes is the promotion and creation of better facilities for cyclists in towns and cities.

The C2C also takes in fantastic scenery. The mountains of the Lake District yield to the subtler but equally beautiful Eden Valley, around Penrith. A stiff climb onto the rolling Pennines provides a further contrast. Settlements are relatively few hereabouts and winter weather can be the most extreme on the whole route. Former lead mining settlements such as Allenheads provide opportunities for sleep and refreshment whilst the landscape also bears reminders of the defunct lead mining industry in the form of old shafts, flues and numerous other constructions. Although the north-east is known perhaps too much for unemployment as a result of heavy industrial decline it has splendid visitor attractions and remarkable architecture

(Newcastle especially). The Wearmouth and Tyne bridges, in Sunderland and Newcastle respectively, are fittingly dramatic heralds to the two finishing points. It's hardly surprising, then, that after negotiating two of the country's main mountain ranges and at least one major city, and linking the Irish and North Seas in the process, that a real sense of achievement in completing this epic journey is just about inevitable!

SUSTRANS - THE CYCLE PATH CHARITY

Sustrans is short for sustainable transport and it is through the construction of an 8,000 mile National Cycle Network that this organisation hopes to promote this aim. Since its founding in 1980 Sustrans has seen a spectacular growth in popularity. The C2C is simply one part in the creation of a such a network. Over 40 million pounds of Millennium funds have been earmarked to help in the construction of this cycle network. Sustrans also relies on income from members (see application on page 96). For further details of Sustrans services contact:

SUSTRANS HEAD OFFICE
35 King Street, Bristol BS1 4DZ
(0117) 929 0888   Website: www.sustrans.org.uk

GETTING THERE AND AWAY

The route is designed to be tackled west to east to take advantage of the prevailing wind which means Whitehaven or Workington is the start point for the vast majority who complete the C2C. For rail access see the map overleaf. Both the phoning and booking system for rail services, especially when wanting to take bikes, is rather complex, no doubt due to the massive reorganisation of the railway system in recent years. At the time of press the system was as follows:

● On inter-city services (e.g Leeds to Carlisle) reserving a bike place is necessary and will cost you £3.
● On regional routes (Carlisle to Workington or Whitehaven) there is no charge and bike space is non-reservable. However there is only guaranteed space for two bikes; admission of any more is at the discretion of the guard.
● The position on the Newcastle to Carlisle line is more complex. Operated as a regional railway, bike space is generally non-reservable, except that some peak services do have reservable bike space! The same caveat of a maximum of 2 bikes applies, the guard still having a discretionary option to allow more.
● Once you know your travel times it is advisable to check with the relevant company. To get to a main line you may have to use your regional railway and therefore you will need to make a similar check as to their arrangements.

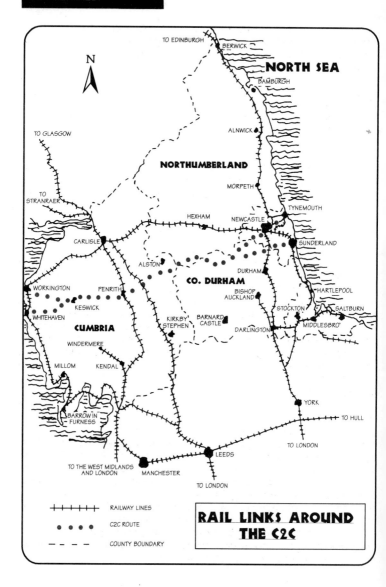

TO EDINBURGH
BERWICK

NORTH SEA

BAMBURGH

TO GLASGOW

ALNWICK

NORTHUMBERLAND

MORPETH

TO STRANRAER

HEXHAM   NEWCASTLE   TYNEMOUTH

CARLISLE   SUNDERLAND

ALSTON   DURHAM

CO. DURHAM

WORKINGTON   PENRITH   BISHOP AUCKLAND   HARTLEPOOL

KESWICK   STOCKTON   SALTBURN

WHITEHAVEN   KIRKBY STEPHEN   BARNARD CASTLE   MIDDLESBRO'

CUMBRIA   DARLINGTON

WINDERMERE

MILLOM   KENDAL

YORK

BARROW IN FURNESS   TO HULL

TO THE WEST MIDLANDS AND LONDON   MANCHESTER   LEEDS   TO LONDON

TO LONDON

++++++   RAILWAY LINES

• • • •   C2C ROUTE

– – –   COUNTY BOUNDARY

RAIL LINKS AROUND THE C2C

British Rail Times and Fares (Inter-city routes) (0345) 484950
North West Railways (Carlisle to Whitehaven) (0161) 2285906
Regional Railways North East (Newcastle to Carlisle and Sunderland to Newcastle) (0113) 2479724

● Trains from Tynemouth to Newcastle are part of the Newcastle Metro system and do not take bikes. It is therefore necessary to retrace your route back to Newcastle Central station. If heading back to Whitehaven from Sunderland you will have to cycle or get the local train back to Newcastle.
● There are a number of **companies** that offer motorised backup::

The Sherpa Van Project operates on a number of long distance trails (0181) 5694101. Website - www.sherpavan.com
The Bike Bus (cycle collection / delivery) Stanley Taxis, Stanley (01207) 237424
Holiday Lakeland, Ireby nr Keswick (016973) 71871
Bike Ride Support Services (0191) 3861966

THE REIVERS

This is the name of Sustrans' new cycle route that you will be able to use as a return loop from May 1998. It will run north of the C2C and will allow those with enough time and energy to make a circular trip without the use of train, car or specialised bus service should you need to get you and your bike back to your start point. You will be able to travel back from Tynemouth to your start point in the west, via the Kielder Forest area and Carlisle. Or, of course, you can return another time to complete 'The Reivers'. Now the subject of an 'Ultimate' guide from Excellent Books.

SIGNING ON THE C2C

Many difficult junctions on the C2C have been waymarked by Sustrans. The direction sign with the red number seven on it (shown on the front cover) will replace the original, simpler blue sign shortly, so you may come across either version of the sign, depending on when you are cycling the route. You may also see other signs along the way; in particular watch out for the sprayed stencil 'C2C' on the road surface and the accompanying arrow. If you are stuck at a junction check on road signs, gates and other nearby objects carefully and also check the tarmac for C2C signs. Also be aware that occasionally some of the signs may have been stolen or may have been twisted or otherwise vandalised, so you should also know where you are on any maps you are using. The red direction tips on the guide's maps have been written to highlight any potentially confusing junctions and any places where signs were missing at the time of writing the guide.

PREPARATION

Although some 'cycle nuts' aim to do the whole route in less than 24 hours the vast majority of C2Cers are holidaying and usually take up to 7 days. Some keen cyclists, especially those with previous experience of the route, complete it over a long weekend. However most people take between 3 and 5 days, depending on experience, fitness and choice of route. This guide is split into 5 'day' sections, ranging from 22 to 31 miles, aimed at novice cyclists or those with plenty of time who want to take in some attractions, with section start and finish points at or near major population centres to ensure plenty of accommodation and other services. It is still advisable to book accommodation as far in advance as practicable; this is especially the case if you are completing the route in summer or you are planning to stay in smaller settlements with only limited accommodation. Those wanting to camp along the way should certainly have some previous cycling experience and allow extra time as the extra weight slows down even the fittest cyclist quite noticeably.

One of the most important factors in preparation is to have a realistic idea of what daily mileage you are comfortable in achieving; remember the C2C has a large range of terrain and difficulty, from the considerable challenge of the Old Coach Road to flat cycle paths, so adjust time estimates accordingly. The route description profile and grade at the beginning of each section give a good idea of what to expect.

CHECKLIST Basic essentials - there is huge range of specialist cycling gear available. The list assumes you are staying B&B.

Clothing (winter / summer options included)
Helmet
High wicking inner layer (doesn't soak up sweat)
Cycle shirt and / or fleece top
Waterproof outer (preferably breathable-
well known makes are Goretex and Ceplex)
Gloves
Padded shorts
Thermal leggings
Tracksuit bottoms
Waterproof trousers
Boots / trainers / cycling shoes
At the least one change of clothing based
on the above
Sun hat / glasses / block

**Tool Kit ('Multi-tools' may
include several of these)**
Small screwdriver
Small adjustable spanner
Allen keys (4,5,6 mm at least)
Puncture kit, spare inner tube
Pump
Spare brake blocks
Strong tape for quick repairs
Small container of chain and
gear lubricant
Chain link extractor

COMPASS
SWISS ARMY

Other Essentials

Guide and maps (see map section)	Bike lights
Water bottle	Money
Telephone contact of friends/family for emergency	Washing kit
	Towel
Toilet paper	Small first aid kit
Survival bag (used to keep warm if stuck in foul weather conditions	Prescribed medication

This list will have obvious additions depending on the person; you may be camping or you may be enough of a mechanic to be able to replace a spare brake cable.

MAINTENANCE

If you set off with a well maintained bike the chances are that you won't need any of the tools or spares you take. A bike in good condition is especially important for such a long distance route. The most basic check should include the following list and if in any doubt about the state of your bike get it checked over properly at a good bike shop.

Important safety checks - do not neglect them!

● **Brake check** - you should only be able to squeeze in front and rear brake levers a centimetre or two and braking response should be nice and sharp. However check brake blocks aren't rubbing on wheel rims, or even worse, tyres.

● **Brake cables** - check that front and rear brake cables are not fraying. If they are replace them immediately.

● **Brake blocks** - check that when you brake the blocks hit only the wheel rim, not the tyre and that there is plenty of wear left in the block.

● **Tyres** - should be inflated to manufacturer's recommended pressure (as a rough guide you should just be able to depress the tyre when squeezing it). Check there is adequate tread.

● Make sure the following are **lubricated**: front and rear brake pivots, moving parts of front and rear gear mechanisms, chain, brake lever pivots, entry and exit points of all cables. Keep well these points well lubricated during the ride.

● Appropriate **screws and bolts** should be tight and you should check all gears are shifting properly.

For a full guide to buying and maintaining a bike see Haynes 'The Bike Book'.

CARRYING LOADS

Panniers are the ideal way to carry your extra gear. Small amounts of gear can be put in bum bags and the smaller seat and frame bags that fit around the bike or in handlebar bags or even a very small backpack. However unless travelling very light in summer you will probably need panniers. Start off with rear panniers which sit on a frame over the rear wheel. Large amounts of extra gear will go in 'low rider' front panniers either side of the front forks. At all costs don't overload handlebar bags or a backpack - this will affect handling and balance dangerously.

USING THIS GUIDE AND OTHER MAPS

Although you should be able to complete the C2C with an up to date edition of this book you are very strongly advised to take other maps. You should at the very least also take the Sustrans C2C map and use it in conjunction with this guide. Amongst many other features this map shows places where you collect Sustrans ink stamps on a card. Ordnance Survey 1:50,000 Landranger maps show even more detail but you will need 5 of these to cover most of the route, which will work out at £20 and a sizeable chunk of valuable storage space. You will also have to highlight the route on the OS maps. The maps you will need are as follows, but are only really feasible for use by a large group who can share the cost and space: Numbers 89 (West Cumbria), 90 (Penrith & Keswick), 86 (Haltwhistle & Brampton), 87 (Hexham & Haltwhistle), 88 (Newcastle, Durham & Sunderland). 'Streetfinder' or 'A to Z' type maps of towns and cities, Sunderland or Newcastle especially, are also helpful. Maps in this book run consecutively, from west to east, so you should be able to follow the route just by turning the pages, without orientation problems.

MAP KEY

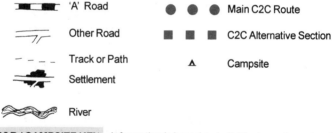

▬▬▬ 'A' Road	● ● ● Main C2C Route
═══╤═ Other Road	■ ■ ■ C2C Alternative Section
– – – – Track or Path	▲ Campsite
━━ Settlement	
～～～ River	

B&B / CAMPSITE KEY Information is based on individual questionnaires from owners; please confirm the information whilst booking.

B&B Abbreviations - prices are per person per night based on a double room.

£ = Under £10   ££ = Under £15   £££ = Under £20   ££££ = Under £25
£££££ = Over £25   ME = Meals   PL = Packed Lunches   DR = Drying Facilities
LAU = Laundry Facilities   SEC = Secure Bike Place   WKSH = Workshop facilites
The distance of the establishment from the route is given lastly, if known.

Campsite Abbreviations

20PL = Number of Tent Places   WC = Toilet Facilities   SH = Shower Facilities
SHP = Shop Facilities   CAF = Cafe Facilities   LAU = Laundry Facilities

OTHER TRAILS USED BY THE C2C

SECTION	TRAIL NAME	TRAIL DETAILS
1A Whitehaven - Keswick	Whitehaven-Ennerdale railway path	14 km - green cast iron signs
1B Workington - Keswick	Workington-Camerton path	5km - no signing apparent
2 Keswick - Penrith	Keswick Railway Path (alternative route)	5km - no signing Beautiful valley path
4 Nenthead - Consett (Runs from Crawleyside to Consett)	Waskerley Way	15km - some signs Interesting transition from moorland to pasture
5A Consett - Sunderland	Consett - Sunderland railway path	34km - dramatic sculptures mark your progress
	River Wear Trail	Followed briefly around James Steel Park and passing under Wearmouth Bridge
5B Consett - Newcastle	Derwent Walk	29km - detour off the Walk opens 1998. Fine wooded trail to the Tyne
	Hadrian's Trail	Currently 5km from the Scotswood Bridge to Swing Bridge in Newcastle. From 1998 will continue on north bank to Tyne Tunnel.
	Keelman's Way	7km. Well-signed interim route from Swing Bridge to Tyne Tunnel (south bank).

11

From the Royal Quays redevelopment area the C2C also coincides with the Waterside Trail, a walking trail that goes as far up the coast as St Mary's lighthouse. It has a distinctive silver triangle / flag motif bearing an abstract design. You leave the trail after descending the steps in North Shields but pick it up again along the bay into Tynemouth. It has interesting information boards.

C2C FACTS*

● The C2C route was opened in 1994 as Sustrans' flagship long distance route
● Around 15,000 people completed the C2C in 1996
● The C2C is intended for cyclists of all abilities to have a go at (though half its users are between 26 and 40 and males outnumber females 3 to 1)
● The most popular choice of route is Whitehaven to Sunderland
● The average cost of a 1996 C2C holiday was estimated at around £100
● The five most popular overnight stays in 1996 were Keswick, Penrith, Alston, Whitehaven and Allenheads
● Most people arrive and depart by car though Sustrans urge people to use the train as being in line with their sustainable transport ideal (see Getting There and Away on page 5)
● 60 % of people stay in B&B accommodation, 21% in tents / camping barns and 12% in Youth Hostels

Many C2Cers thought that certain sections, especially the Old Coach Road (sec. 2) and the climb to Hartside (sec. 3) should have clear warnings published about their difficulty so be warned! Allow plenty of time to complete them and on the Old Coach Road especially be aware it is a very isolated and exposed section of moorland track.

* This information is based on the 1996 report on visitor monitoring on the C2C produced by the University of Sunderland. Thanks to Andy Cope for making the information available for publication.

STOP PRESS

The C2C is currently at an interim stage and changes to the route are steadily taking place. This guide is wire spiral bound. Copies are not bound until distributed to bookshops allowing insertion of stop press changes, so your copy should be up-to-date when bought.

To further ensure that you have current information check with Sustrans you have the most recent map of the route. Why not join Sustrans? Their newsletters will keep you informed of major route changes (see page 96)

1A WHITEHAVEN - KESWICK (OPTION)

Section Distance 31 miles / 50km   **Off-road** 12 miles / 19km

Accumulated Distance 31 miles / 50km

The Route The Whitehaven-Ennerdale cycle path provides a gentle start, passing by several former iron mining villages. The route initially follows the line of a disused rail network that served a myriad of local mines. The true mountains of the Lake District are soon in sight, heralded by pleasant villages such as Lamplugh and High Lorton. After a spectacular climb over the Whinlatter Forest the quaint villages of Braithwaite and Portinscale are accompanied by easy pedaling onto Keswick.

WHITEHAVEN - HISTORY AND ATTRACTIONS

● Listed **'Gem Town'** with well-preserved Georgian architecture. Unusual gridiron street pattern was the first planned town since the middle ages. Many fine buildings. See Roper St. and Lowther St. for good examples.
● Interesting **harbour area** with nearby mine remains of Wellington and Duke Pits at South Beach Recreation Area. Candlestick Chimney viewpoint part of former Wellington pit (operating 1840-1932). Scene of 1910 mine disaster with 136 lives lost.
● The **Beacon Museum** showing the town's connection with slavery, smuggling, mining, shipbuilding and America. Met. Office weather gallery and views over the Solway Firth. Admission charge. (01946) 592302.
● **Michael Moon's Bookshop**, Roper St. - huge selection of second-hand books.
●**St. James Church** has a fine Georgian interior (see map). St. Nicholas Church consists of a fine tower on Lowther St. (drinks and snacks some weekends)

WHITEHAVEN - ACCOMMODATION

Glenlea Country House, Glenlea Hill, Lowca, Whitehaven (01946) 693873 £££-ME- PL-DR-LAU-SEC-WKSH. Approx 5km.
Glenard Guest House, Inkerman Terrace (01946) 692249 ££-ME-PL-DR-SEC-WKSH. 0.25 miles.
Lismore Guest House, Wellington Row (01946) 66028 ££-PL-DR-LAU-SEC. Near route.
Tarn Flatt Hall, Sandwith (01946) 692162 B&B-£££ Camping Barn-£3-ME PL(with B&B only)-DR-SEC. 2 miles.
Tivoli Guest House, 156 Queen St (01946) 67400 ££-PL-SEC. Near route.

13

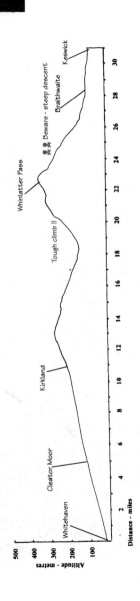

WHITEHAVEN - KESWICK
GRADIENT DIFFICULTY - TOUGH

14

St. Nicholas' Church, Whitehaven

Cross Georgian Guest House, Sneckyeat Rd, Henshingham (01946) 63716 ££(£)-PL-SEC. 1 mile from start. Parking facilities for those leaving cars and returning after completion of route.
Also try: Brunos Hotel, 9-11 Church St. (01946) 65270 **Corkickle Guest House**, 1 Corkickle (01946) 692073 **Waverley Hotel**, Tangier St. (01946) 694337

WHITEHAVEN - OTHER FACILITIES

Tourist Information Market Hall, Market Place (01946) 852939
Market Days Thursday and Saturday
Early Closing Wednesday
Hospital West Cumberland Hospital, Henshingham (01946) 693181
Police (01946) 692616
Banks Barclays Bank, Strand St. Cashpoint - Midland Bank, 69 Lowther St. Cashpoint - NatWest, 71 Lowther St. Cashpoint
Cycle Shops Mark Taylor Cycles, 5-6 New St. (01946) 692252 Camskill Cycles, Pottery Rd. , off Coach Rd. (01946) 694794 ⚲ Ainfield Cycle Centre, Cleator (01946) 812427

WHITEHAVEN TO KESWICK

●**Cleator Moor and Cleator** Modern miners memorial sculpture in market square. Besides Cleator's Roman Catholic church is St. Mary's grotto. Attracts thousands of pilgrims each year. The Crown, Bowthorn Rd, Cleator. Lunch 11-4.30. Dinner 7-11. Under £5. Robinsons and Hartleys.
●**Arlecdon/Rowrah** The Hound Inn, Parks Rd, Lunch 12-2 Dinner 5.30-8.30 £5-£10 John Smiths, Theakstons, Youngers. Sun Inn, Lunch 12-2 Evening meals 6-9 £5-10 Tetleys, Jennings, guest beers.
●**Ennerdale Bridge** Shepherds Arms Hotel,Lunch 12-2 Teas 3-6 Dinner 7-9.20. Upwards of £5. Thorntons and Beamish.
● **Lamplugh** ▲ Inglenook Caravan Park (01946) 861240 6PL-WC-SH-SHP. Public cafe at Dockray Caravan Park opposite.
●**Loweswater** Picturesque village with church, next to route. Kirkstile Inn Meals 12-9 £5-£10 Jennings, Cumberland Ale.
●**Low Lorton** Lorton Hall (private) has fifteenth century pele tower. Wheatsheaf Inn - enquire about camping facilities. ▲ Whinfell Hall Farm (01900) 85260 30PL- WC-SH March-October
● **High Lorton** Yew Tree behind village hall was George Fox's preaching place. Former home of Jennings brewery - see information sign near post office.
●**Whinlatter Pass** Forest Enterprise runs Whinlatter Visitor Centre. Good displays for all ages and cafe. Signed walks to Lord's Seat and Barf viewpoints. (017687) 78469 ⚲ Rivelin Moss Cycle Hire on route before visitor centre.

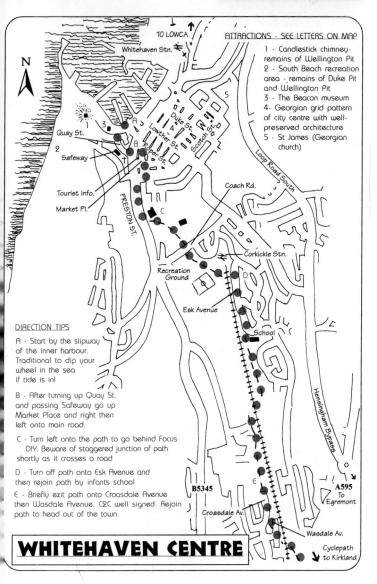

ATTRACTIONS - SEE LETTERS ON MAP

1 - Candlestick chimney - remains of Wellington Pit
2 - South Beach recreation area - remains of Duke Pit and Wellington Pit
3 - The Beacon museum
4 - Georgian grid pattern of city centre with well-preserved architecture
5 - St James (Georgian church)

DIRECTION TIPS

A - Start by the slipway of the inner harbour. Traditional to dip your wheel in the sea if tide is in!

B - After turning up Quay St. and passing Safeway go up Market Place and right then left onto main road.

C - Turn left onto the path to go behind Focus DIY. Beware of staggered junction of path shortly as it crosses a road

D - Turn off path onto Esk Avenue and then rejoin path by infants school

E - Briefly exit path onto Croasdale Avenue then Wasdale Avenue. C2C well signed. Rejoin path to head out of the town.

WHITEHAVEN CENTRE

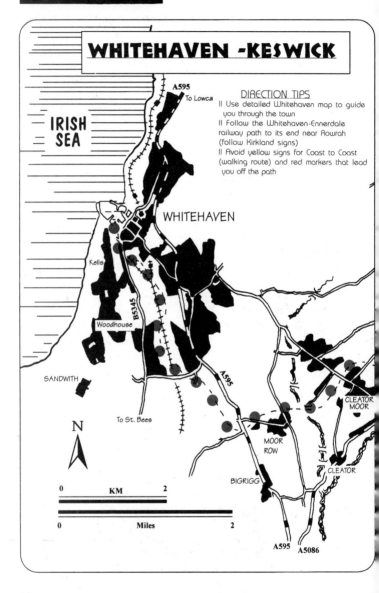

WHITEHAVEN -KESWICK

A595
To Lowca

IRISH SEA

WHITEHAVEN

DIRECTION TIPS

ll Use detailed Whitehaven map to guide you through the town
ll Follow the Whitehaven-Ennerdale railway path to its end near Rowrah (follow Kirkland signs)
ll Avoid yellow signs for Coast to Coast (walking route) and red markers that lead you off the path

Kells

B5345

Woodhouse

SANDWITH

To St. Bees

N

A595

MOOR ROW

CLEATOR MOOR

CLEATOR

BIGRIGG

0   KM   2

0   Miles   2

A595 A5086

18

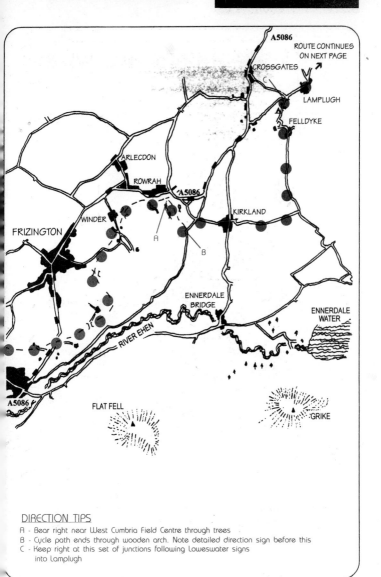

ROUTE CONTINUES ON NEXT PAGE →

DIRECTION TIPS

A - Bear right near West Cumbria Field Centre through trees
B - Cycle path ends through wooden arch. Note detailed direction sign before this
C - Keep right at this set of junctions following Loweswater signs
    into Lamplugh

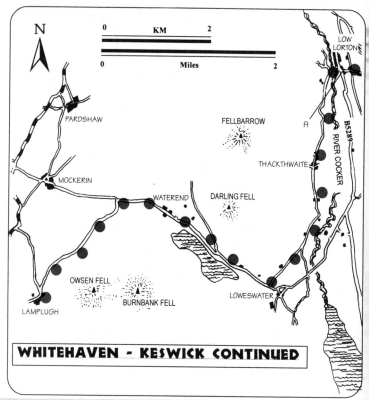

WHITEHAVEN - KESWICK CONTINUED

B&Bs / Youth Hostels (Whitehaven to Keswick)

How Hall Farm, Ennerdale, Cleator (01946) 861266 £££-ME-PL-DR-SEC. 2 miles.
Shepherds Arms Hotel, Ennerdale Bridge (01946) 861249 £££££-ME-PL-DR-LAU-SEC. 1 mile from route (turn right at Kirkland).
Graythwaite, Loweswater (01946) 861555 £££-ME-PL-DR-LAU-SEC-WKSH. 0.5 miles.
Kirkstile Inn, Loweswater (01900) 85219 ££££-ME-PL-DR-LAU-SEC-WKSH. 500 yds.
Meadow Bank, High Lorton (01900) 85315 £££-PL-DR-LAU-SEC-WKSH. 200 yds.
Swallow Barn (Camping Barn), Waterend Farm, Loweswater (017687) 72803 £

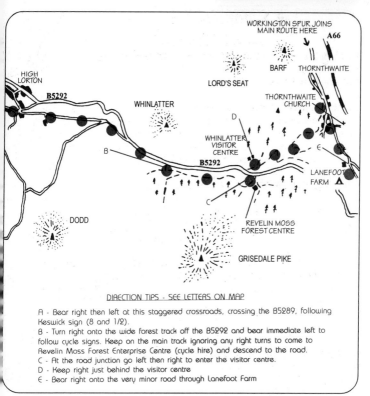

WORKINGTON SPUR JOINS
MAIN ROUTE HERE A66

BARF THORNTHWAITE

LORD'S SEAT

HIGH
LORTON

B5292

WHINLATTER

THORNTHWAITE
CHURCH

D

WHINLATTER
VISITOR
CENTRE

B

B5292

E

LANEFOOT
FARM

C

DODD

REVELIN MOSS
FOREST CENTRE

GRISEDALE PIKE

DIRECTION TIPS - SEE LETTERS ON MAP

A - Bear right then left at this staggered crossroads, crossing the B5289, following Keswick sign (8 and 1/2).
B - Turn right onto the wide forest track off the B5292 and bear immediate left to follow cycle signs. Keep on the main track ignoring any right turns to come to Revelin Moss Forest Enterprise Centre (cycle hire) and descend to the road.
C - At the road junction go left then right to enter the visitor centre.
D - Keep right just behind the visitor centre
E - Bear right onto the very minor road through Lanefoot Farm

Terrace Farm, High Lorton (01900) 85278 £££-DR-SEC. 0.25 miles. March - Oct.
Cottage in the Wood Hotel, Whinlatter Pass (017687) 78409 ££££-PL-DR-SEC-WKSH. On route. Dinner £16.50 5 courses. Bar (Boddingtons).

Ennerdale Youth Hostel, Cat Crag, Ennerdale (01946) 861237 Evening meal. Self-catering kitchen. Limited shop. Gas only. ££.

Also try: Ennerdale Country House Hotel (01946) 813907 **Beckfoot,** Ennerdale (01946) 861235

NOTE - FOR THORNTHWAITE-KESWICK DETAILS SEE PAGE 28 AND FOLLOWING.

1B WORKINGTON - KESWICK

Section Distance 25 miles / 40 km   **Off-road** 7 miles / 11km

Accumulated Distance 25 miles / 40km

The Route Workington is still a working port and the harbour area is still dominated by heavy industry. Despite losing out to Whitehaven in this respect the section has advantages; it is shorter and with more gentle gradients and offers the chance to visit the historic market town of Cockermouth. Note that at the time of writing the Workington - Keswick section had very few C2C signs.

WORKINGTON - HISTORY AND ATTRACTIONS

● The **Helena Thompson Museum** is based around local collections. Includes social and industrial history of Workington, once world famous for coal, ship building and steel. Housed in a fine Georgian building. Free admission. Park End Road. (01900) 62598
● **Workington Hall** Imposing ruin and former home of local Lords of the Manor the Curwens who built up the local coal industry. Full cork model in Helena Thompson Museum. Admission charge. (01900) 604351

WORKINGTON ACCOMMODATION

Osbourne House 31 Brow Top (01900) 603400 £££-ME-PL-DR-LAU-SEC. 0.8km
Boston Guest House, 1 St. Michaels Rd. (01900) 603435 £££-SEC. 1.5 miles.
Morven House Hotel, Siddick Rd. (01900) 602118 £££-ME-PL-DR-LAU-SEC-WKSH. 1 mile from start.
Sunny House, Asby nr. Workington (01946) 861934 ££-PL-DR-SEC-WKSH. 1 mile.
Appletree Inn, 31 Finkle St. (01900) 871160 ££-ME(Pub attached)-PL-DR-SEC-WKSH. 1 mile.

WORKINGTON - OTHER INFORMATION

Market Days Wednesday and Saturday
Early closing Thursday
Hospital Workington Infirmary, Infirmary Rd. (01900) 602244
Banks Midland, 3 Pow St. Cashpoint. - Natwest, 31 Pow St. Cashpoint.
Bike Shops Traffic Lights Bikes, 35 Washington St (01900) 603283 New bike Shop, 18-20 Market Place (01900) 603337

WORKINGTON - COCKERMOUTH

● **Camerton** Pretty church on banks of Derwent. Black Tom Inn. No meals.
● **Great Broughton** Christ Church pretty village church. The Brewery House pub.
● **Papcastle** Former site of a Roman fort, now a pleasant village.

COCKERMOUTH - HISTORY AND ATTRACTIONS

● Only one of two listed **'Gem Towns'** in Cumbria (Whitehaven is the other).
● **Wordsworth House**. Home of William and Dorothy Wordsworth. National Trust owned with cafe. Admission fee to non-members. Seasonal variations in opening. (01900) 824805
● **Printing House Museum**. Unusual display of printing technology through the ages. 'Hands on' experience. Admission charge. (01900) 824984
● **Aspects of Motoring Museum**. Motoring through the ages. Admission charge. Closed Jan. Restricted opening Feb. (01900) 824448
● **Toy and Model Museum**. Admission charge. Open Feb-Nov. (01900) 827606
● **Statue of R.Mayo** in main street. Former town MP and only Viceroy of India ever assassinated.
● **Jennings Brewery Tour**. Working brewery. Admission charge. (01900) 823214

COCKERMOUTH - ACCOMMODATION

Albany House Wordsworth Terrace, Windmill Lane (01900) 825630
££££-PL-DR-LAU-SEC. 0.5km.
Castlegate Guest House 6 Castlegate (01900) 826749 £££-PL-LAU-SEC. Near route.
Rook Guest House, 9 Castlegate (01900) 828496 £££-PL-DR-LAU-SEC-Basic tools. Near route.
Rose Cottage, Lorton Rd (01900) 822189 £££-ME-PL-DR-LAU-SEC. 0.5 miles.
Benson Court Cottage, 10 St Helens St. (01900) 822303 ££-DR-LAU nearby-SEC. Very near route.
The Old Vicarage, Lorton Rd (01900) 828505 £££-SEC-WKSH. 3.75 miles.

Hundith Hill Hotel, Lorton Vale (01900) 822092 ££££-ME-PL-DR-SEC. basic tools. About 0.6 km from route to SE of Cockermouth off the B5292.

Cockermouth Youth Hostel Double Mills (01900) 822561 Evening meal-self catering-cycle shed-all day access. ££. Near route.

COCKERMOUTH - OTHER INFORMATION

Tourist Information Town Hall, Market St. (01900) 822634
Market Days Monday including livestock auction.
Early Closing Thursday
Hospital Cockermouth Cottage Hospital (01900) 822226
Banks Barclays, 30 Main St. Cashpoint. - Midland, 1 Main St. Cashpoint.
Bike Shops Wordsworth Hotel Bike Hire (01900) 822757 Derwent Cycles, 4 Market Place (01900) 822113

COCKERMOUTH - KESWICK

● **Wythop Mill** Interesting hamlet right next to the mill. (017687) 76394 Small water-powered mill originally for corn grinding, then woodworking tools. Includes coffee shop with meals. Good Friday-Oct. Admission charge.
● **Embleton village** Wheatsheaf Pub. Lunch 12-2. Evening meals 6-9. £5-£10. Jennings.

Village charm at Wythop Mill

WORKINGTON - KESWICK

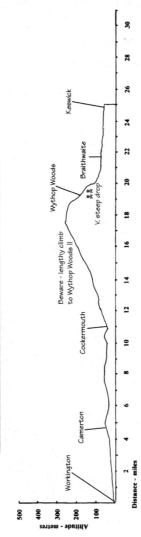

25

WORKINGTON CENTRE

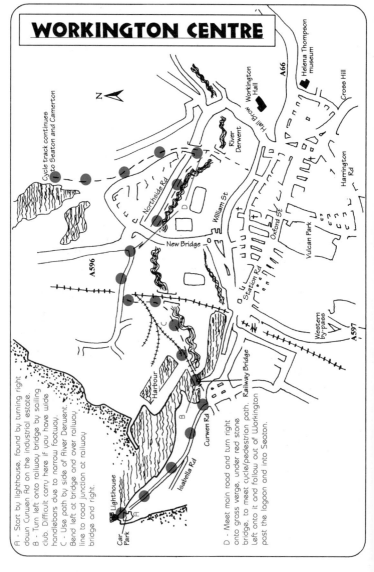

A - Start by lighthouse, found by turning right down Curwen Rd on the industrial estate.
B - Turn left onto railway bridge by sailing club. Difficult carry here if you have wide handlebars due to narrow footway.
C - Use path by side of River Derwent. Bend left at bridge and over railway line to road junction at railway bridge and right.

D - Meet main road and turn right onto grass verge, under red stone bridge, to meet cycle/pedestrian path. Railway Bridge Left onto it and follow out of Workington past the lagoon and into Seaton.

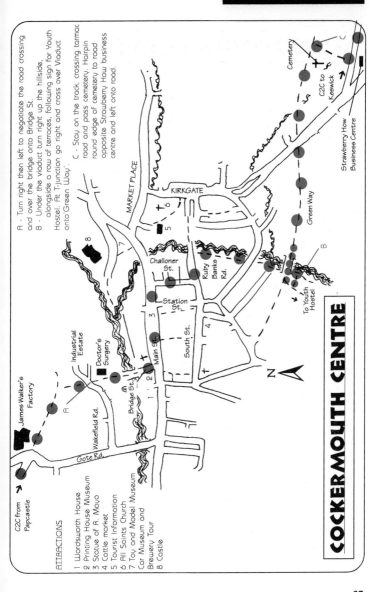

A - Turn right then left to negotiate the road crossing and over the bridge onto Bridge St.

B - Under the viaduct turn right up the hillside, alongside a row of terraces, following sign for Youth Hostel. At T-junction go right and cross over Viaduct onto 'Green Way'.

C - Stay on the track, crossing tarmac road and pass cemetery. Hairpin round edge of cemetery to road opposite Strawberry How business centre and left onto road.

ATTRACTIONS
1 Wordsworth House
2 Printing House Museum
3 Statue of R. Mayo
4 Cattle market
5 Tourist Information
6 All Saints Church
7 Toy and Model Museum
Car Museum and
Brewery Tour
8 Castle

COCKERMOUTH CENTRE

27

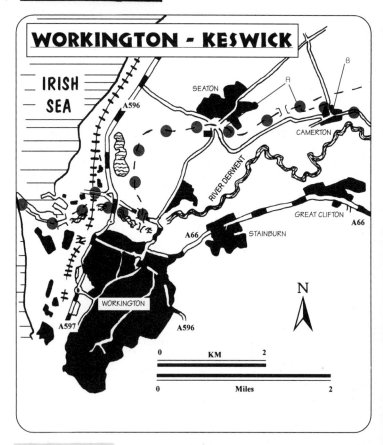

WORKINGTON - KESWICK

AROUND KESWICK

THE FOLLOWING LISTINGS ARE COMMON TO 1A AND 1B - THEY ARE ON THE ROUTE AFTER THE SECTIONS HAVE JOINED.

● **Thornthwaite** Note 'The Bishop'; whitewashed rock pinnacle opposite Swan Hotel. Painted yearly by hotel landlord.
▲ Lanefoot Camping (017687) 78315 WC

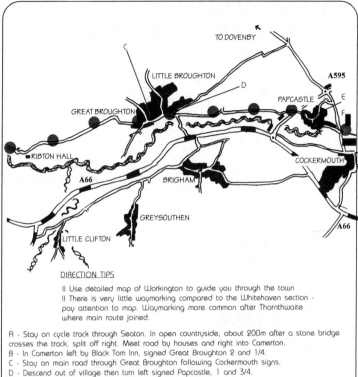

TO DOVENBY

LITTLE BROUGHTON

A595

PAPCASTLE

GREAT BROUGHTON

COCKERMOUTH

RIBTON HALL

A66

BRIGHAM

GREYSOUTHEN

A66

LITTLE CLIFTON

DIRECTION TIPS

!! Use detailed map of Workington to guide you through the town
!! There is very little waymarking compared to the Whitehaven section - pay attention to map. Waymarking more common after Thornthwaite where main route joined.

A - Stay on cycle track through Seaton. In open countryside, about 200m after a stone bridge crosses the track, split off right. Meet road by houses and right into Camerton.

B - In Camerton left by Black Tom Inn, signed Great Broughton 2 and 1/4.

C - Stay on main road through Great Broughton following Cockermouth signs.

D - Descend out of village then turn left signed Papcastle, 1 and 3/4.

E - Ignore left for Carlisle in Papcastle.

F - Cross main road onto path by James Walker's factory then consult town centre map.

● **Braithwaite** Quiet village with nice centre. Shop. **Coledale Inn** Lunch 12-2 Bar meals 6.30-9.00. £5-£10 Youngers, Yates, Jennings, Theakstons. **Royal Oak Inn** Lunch 12-2 Bar meals 6-9. £5 and up. Jennings ales and other real ales.

🚲 Spares and repairs listed on the route, just past village shop (signed).

⚠ Braithwaite Bridges (017687) 78343 100PL-WC-SH-SHP-CAF-March-Nov

⚠ Scotgate Caravan Park (017687) 78343 150PL-WC-SH-SHP-CAF-LAUN-March-November

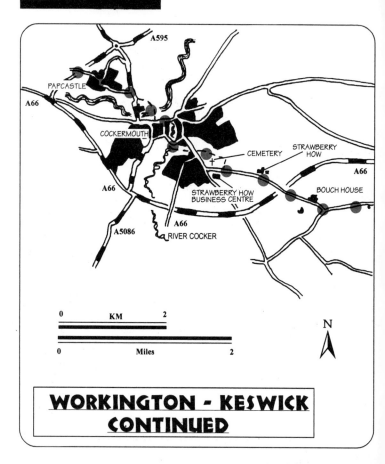

WORKINGTON - KESWICK CONTINUED

●**Portinscale** Elegant villa settlement next door to Keswick despite its name deriving from the Norse for prostitute's hut! Shop. **Lingholme Gardens** Formal gardens and woodlands nearby with tea room. April-Oct.

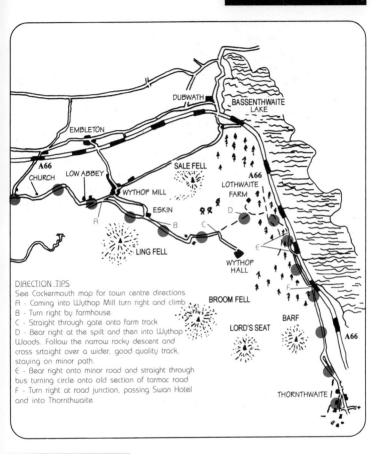

DUBWATH

BASSENTHWAITE LAKE

EMBLETON

SALE FELL

A66
CHURCH   LOW ABBEY

A66
LOTHWAITE FARM

WYTHOP MILL

ESKIN

A

B

C

D

LING FELL

WYTHOP HALL

E

BROOM FELL

BARF

LORD'S SEAT

A66

THORNTHWAITE

DIRECTION TIPS

See Cockermouth map for town centre directions
A - Coming into Wythop Mill turn right and climb
B - Turn right by farmhouse
C - Straight through gate onto farm track
D - Bear right at the spilt and then into Wythop
Woods. Follow the narrow rocky descent and
cross srtaight over a wider, good quality track,
staying on minor path.
E - Bear right onto minor road and straight through
bus turning circle onto old section of tarmac road
F - Turn right at road junction, passing Swan Hotel
and into Thornthwaite

B&Bs - Around Keswick

Uzzicar Farm, Newlands (South of Little Braithwaite) (017687) 78367 ££--PL-DR-SEC. 1 mile.
Also try the following around Braithwaite: Coledale Inn (017687) 78272 **Ivy House Hotel** (017687) 78338 **Maple Bank Country Guest House** (017687) 78229 **Middle Ruddings Country Inn** (017687) 78436

KESWICK CENTRE

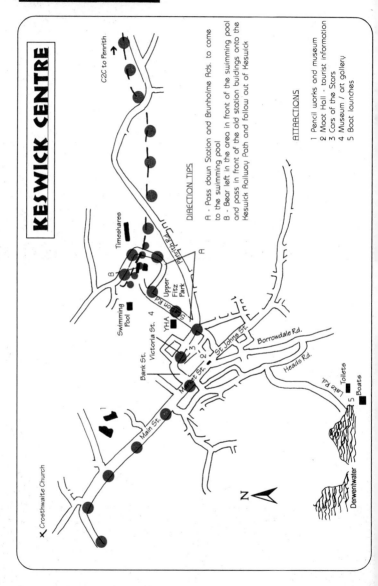

C2C to Penrith

DIRECTION TIPS

A - Pass down Station and Brunholme Rds. to come to the swimming pool

B - Bear left in the area in front of the swimming pool and pass in front of the old station buildings onto the Keswick Railway Path and follow out of Keswick

ATTRACTIONS

1 Pencil works and museum
2 Moot Hall - tourist information
3 Cars of the Stars
4 Museum / art gallery
5 Boat launches

Keswick Railway Path

Timeshares

Swimming Pool

Upper Fitz Park

Station Rd.

Bank St.

Victoria St.

YHA

St Johns St.

Borrowdale Rd.

Heads Rd.

Lake Rd.

Toilets

Boats

Main St.

Crosthwaite Church

N

Derwentwater

C2C LANDSCAPES

Above: The start of the Old Coach Road section (section 2)
Below: Approaching Wythop Woods (section 1B)

Above: The alternative route via Ramshaw (section 4)
Below: The Northern Pennines from the Old Coach Rd (section 2)
Opposite: Rolling moors approaching Allenheads (section 4)

Above: A quiet break after climbing out of Allenheads (section 4)
Below: Crossing the River Wear near Cox Green (section 5A)

C2C START AND FINISH   Above: Whitehaven harbour (section 1A)
Below: Collingwood's Monument at Tynemouth (section 5B)
Previous Page: Approachinhg C2C start at Workington (section 1B)

Above: Wearmouth Bridge, Sunderland (section 5A)
Below: The famous bridges over the Tyne, Newcastle (section 5B)

C2C ANCIENT & MODERN
Above: Castlerigg Stone Circle (section 2)
Below: Sculpture at the new university campus, Riverside, Sunderland (section 5A)

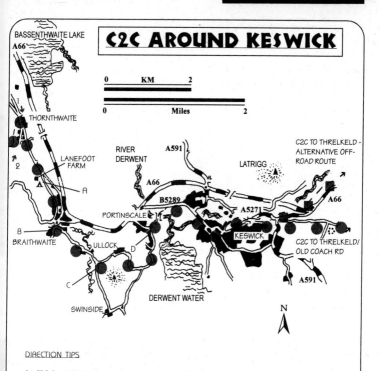

C2C AROUND KESWICK

BASSENTHWAITE LAKE
A66

THORNTHWAITE

LANEFOOT FARM

RIVER DERWENT

A591

A66

B5289

PORTINSCALE

BRAITHWAITE

ULLOCK

SWINSIDE

DERWENT WATER

LATRIGG

C2C TO THRELKELD - ALTERNATIVE OFF-ROAD ROUTE

A66

A5271

KESWICK

C2C TO THRELKELD/ OLD COACH RD

A591

N

0   KM   2

0   Miles   2

DIRECTION TIPS

1- C2C from Workington   2 - C2C from Whitehaven
A - Turn onto minor road through Lanefoot Fm. Easy to miss.
B - Straight over crossroads in Braithwaite to Ivy House Hotel.
C - Follow signs for Ullock.
D - Bear right by Derwent Water Hotel in Portinscale. Dismount to cross Derwent footbridge.

2 KESWICK - PENRITH

Section Distance 22 miles / 35km   **Off-road** 2 miles / 3km
(The Old Coach Road is a 5mile / 8km tough off-road option)

Accumulated Distance From Whitehaven 55 miles / 88km
From Workington 47 miles / 76 km

The Route The high summits of the Lake District are left behind as you approach the flatter more pastoral country of the Eden Valley, with its accent on quiet market towns and glorious woodlands contrasting to the large-scale tourism of the Lake District. Although the main route is relatively flat the off-road option along the Old Coach Road is a serious challenge as the exposed rocky track.climbs high onto Threlkeld Common, whilst the main route gently undulates along the valley bottom. The other off-road alternative is the delightful Keswick railway path. After a couple of steep gradients it turns into an easy trip through thick woods, crossing and re-crossing the River Greta over a series of charming bridges to bring you to Threlkeld.

KESWICK - HISTORY AND ATTRACTIONS

● Established as a mining centre and market town, it quickly became a Victorian tourist centre, amidst glorious Lakeland scenery. Remains the main **tourist centre** in the Northern Lakes.
● A number of interesting buildings include the **Moot Hall** (tourist info. building) and **Crosthwaite Church** with panoramic viewfinder. Southey's grave and consecration crosses inside and outside the building.
●**Keswick Museum and Art Gallery** Interesting and unusual collection of objects in traditional style museum. Admission charge. (017687) 73263
● **Pencil Museum** World's largest pencil and other offbeat pencil information. Admission charge. (017687) 73626
●**Cars of the Stars** Including the Batmobile, Chitty Chitty Bang Bang and others. (017687) 73757. Easter-Nov then restricted opening.
●**Derwentwater Boat Trips** Calling at the main points of interest around the lake. Admission charge. (017687) 72263
● **George Fisher** Huge stock of outdoor activity goods. Borrowdale Rd.

KESWICK - ACCOMMODATION

Glamamara Guest House, 9 Acorn St (017687) 73216 £££-DR-LAU (nearby)-SEC-WKSH. Caters especially for cyclists as it runs cycle hire (see below). 0.8km

KESWICK - PENRITH
GRADIENT DIFFICULTY - EASY
(OLD COACH RD OPTION VERY TOUGH)

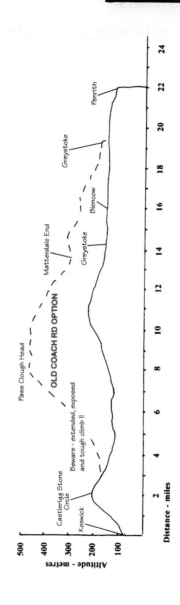

35

Brooklyn House, Penrith Rd (017687) 72870 £££-PL-SEC-WKSH. Near route.
Sandon Guest House, Southey St (017687) 73648 £££-ME-PL-LAU nearby-SEC. 500yds.
Rivendell, 23 Helvellyn St (017687) 73822 £££-ME-PL-DR-LAU nearby-SEC-WKSH. Near route.
Pitcairn House, 7 Blencathra St (017687) 72453 ££-ME-PL-DR-SEC-Some tools. 0.25 miles.
Beckside Guest House, 5 Wordsworth St (017687) 73093 £££-ME-PL-DR-LAU (close by)-SEC. 500 yds.
Keswick Youth Hostel, Station Road (017687) 74129 £-ME-PL-DR-LAU-SEC. On route.

OTHER INFORMATION - KESWICK

Tourist Information Moot Hall, Market Place (017687) 72645
Market Days Saturday
Early Closing Wednesday
Banks All the following have cashpoints: Barclays, Market Sq. Lloyds, 4 Main St. Natwest, 28 Main St.
Cycle Shops Glamamara Guest House Cycle Hire On C2C, B5289, coming onto Keswick. Also spares and repairs. (017687) 75255. Keswick Mountain Bikes, Southey Hill. (017687) 74492.

Lakeland view on the route near Ullock

KESWICK TO PENRITH - MAIN ROUTE

● **Castlerigg Stone Circle** One of 40 stone circles in Cumbria but arguably the one with the most amazing setting. Thought to date from around 3000B.C. Built by a large team of men, it was possibly a meeting or trading place for Neolithic society, although this is largely presumption.

● **Threlkeld** Former mining community with tuberculosis sanitorium built nearby. White Horse Inn Lunch 12-2 Dinner 6.45-9.00 £5-£10 Jennings Best and Blencathra. ▲Setmabanning Farm (017687) 79229 20PL-WC-SH-DRY. March-Oct.

Threlkeld Quarry and Mining Museum (017687) 79747 Off the B5322 south of the route in the old quarries. Huge geology book collection for sale. Easter to Oct and winter weekends. Admission charge.

● **Walthwaite** ▲ Hutton Moor End Farm. (017687) 79615-15PL-WC-SH-DRY. March-October.

● **Troutbeck** Pub ▲Gill Head Farm. (017687) 79652-25PL-WC-SH-SHP-LAU-DRY. March-Oct. ▲ Troutbeck Head Camp Site. (017687) 83521-WC-SH-SHP-LAU-DRY. March-Oct.

● **Greystoke** Compact centre based around village green. Impressive entrance to private castle and market cross. Interesting church. *Tarzan of the Apes* modelled on Lord Greystoke. Cafe. Pub.

● **Blencow** Before entering Blencow look for the hall on the left with modern house built into ruined defensive pele towers.

B&Bs - Keswick - Penrith. Main route.

Scales Farm Country Guest House, Scales, Threlkeld (017687) 79660 ££££-PL-DR-SEC-Basic tools. Near route.

Blease Farm, Blease Rd, Threlkeld (017687) 79087 ££££-PL-DR-LAU-SEC-WKSH. 0.3 miles.

Gill Head, Troutbeck. Contact as for campsite above. £££-ME-PL-DR-LAU-SEC-WKSH. On route

Whitbarrow Farm, Berrier (017684) 83366 £££-PL-DR-SEC. 500yds.

Motherby House, Motherby nr Greystoke (017684) 83368 ££-ME-PL-DR-LAU-SEC. 1.5 miles.

Lattendales Farm Berrier Rd, Greystoke (017684) 83474 ££-DR-SEC-WKSH. Near route.

Meledene, Icold Rd, Greystoke (017684) 83856 ££-PL-DR-SEC. Near route.

Orchard Cottage, Church Rd, Greystoke (017684) 83264 £££-PL-DR-LAU-SEC-WKSH. 100 yds.

Little Blencow Farm, Blencow (017684) 83338 £££-PL-DR-LAU-SEC-WKSH. On route.

37

Crown Inn, Blencow (017684) 83369 £££-ME (pub attached)-PL-SEC-Basic tools.
On route. Bar meals 7-9 everyday. Lunches 12-2 weekends. £5-£10. Directors cask,
Theakstons.

OLD COACH ROAD OPTION - ST. JOHNS IN THE VALE - GREYSTOKE.

Great Dockray White Horse Inn. Lunch 12-2.30 Dinner 5.30-8.30 (Sun 7-8.30)
£5-6. John Smiths, Theakstons, Scotch, Guinness.

B&BS / Hotels - Old Coach Road option

Thackthwaite Under Mell House, Thackthwaite village (017684) 86397 £££-SEC.
250yds.

PENRITH - HISTORY AND ATTRACTIONS

● Beautiful red **sandstone market town,** historically the target of Scottish border
raids. Series of market places connected by narrow streets show desire for security
against the Scots.
● **Penrith Beacon** A hilltop structure used through the ages to warn of the threat
of invasion. Present structure dates from 1719. Accessible by foot. Signed at junction
at top of Fell Lane.
●**Robinson's School** Former charitable provider of education now housing tourist
information and small museum. No charge. (01768) 212228
● **St. Andrew's Church** Set in fine architecture of Bishop's Yard. Medieval tower
with Georgian nave. Unusual 'Giant's Grave' in churchyard (arrangement of ancient
crosses and hogback graves) near Gothic monument to Robert Virtue (railway
engineer).
● **Castle ruins** Began in the fourteenth century and later occupied by Richard
Duke of Gloucester as 'Guardian of the West march towards Scotland'.
● **Musgrave Monument** Erected 1851 by public subscription as a memorial on
the early death of son of Sir George and Lady Musgrave.
● Many other **fine buildings** such as the Mansion House and Town Hall.

PENRITH - ACCOMMODATION

Glendale Guest House, 4 Portland Place (01768) 862579 £££-PL-DR-LAU-SEC-
WKSH. On route
Brandelhow Guest House, 1 Portland Place (01768) 864470 £££-PL-DR-SEC.
On route.
7 Alexandra Rd (01768) 863950 ££-PL-SEC. Near route.
The Friarage, Friargate (01768) 863635 £££-DR-LAU-SEC. Near route.

Victoria Guest House, 3 Victoria Rd. (01768) 891399 £££-PL-DR-LAU nearby.
Near route.
Caledonia Guest House, 8 Victoria Rd (01768) 864482 £££-PL-DR-LAU nearby-
SEC. 0.5 mile.
Albany House, 5 Portland Place (01768) 863072 £££-PL-DR-SEC-Basic tools.
Near route.
Ash Grove, Alexandra Road (01768) 864353 £££-DR-LAU-SEC.

Starting to climb on the Old Coach Road alternative route

KESWICK - PENRITH

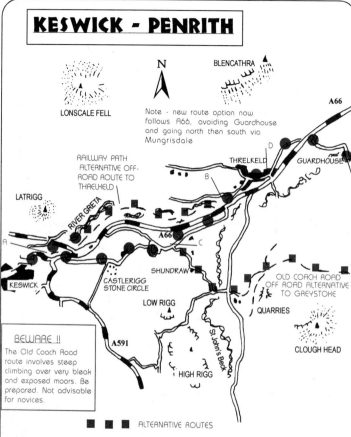

LONSCALE FELL

BLENCATHRA

N

Note - new route option now follows A66, avoiding Guardhouse and going north then south via Mungrisdale

A66

THRELKELD

GUARDHOUSE

RAILWAY PATH ALTERNATIVE OFF-ROAD ROUTE TO THRELKELD

LATRIGG

RIVER GRETA

A66

D

B

A

KESWICK

CASTLERIGG STONE CIRCLE

SHUNDRAW

C

OLD COACH ROAD OFF ROAD ALTERNATIVE TO GREYSTOKE

LOW RIGG

QUARRIES

St John's Beck

CLOUGH HEAD

BEWARE !!

The Old Coach Road route involves steep climbing over very bleak and exposed moors. Be prepared. Not advisable for novices.

A591

HIGH RIGG

■ ■ ■ ALTERNATIVE ROUTES

DIRECTION TIPS

A - EASY TO MISS! On the main road pass under the main road and then double back to turn left onto it. Turn right on minor right signed 'Castlerigg Stone Circle'. Otherwise continue straight on to follow alternative route. CAUTION - steep climb and descent on alternative route after passing under dual corrigeway.

B - Emerge from railway path and left down side of A66. Take next left for Threlkeld.

C - For Old Coach Road alternative route take right here for Shundraw.

D - Turn left up Fell Side, marked dead end then cross A66 and turn for Guardhouse.

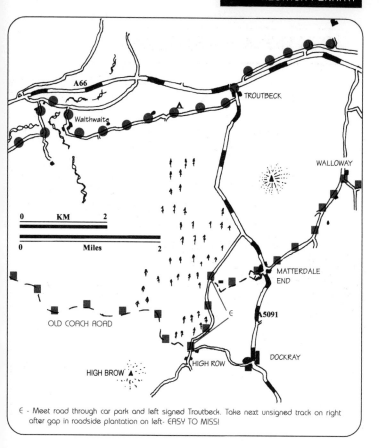

A66

Walthwaite

TROUTBECK

WALLOWAY

0   KM   2

0   Miles   2

OLD COACH ROAD

MATTERDALE
END

€

A5091

DOCKRAY

HIGH BROW ▲

HIGH ROW

€ - Meet road through car park and left signed Troutbeck. Take next unsigned track on right after gap in roadside plantation on left- EASY TO MISS!

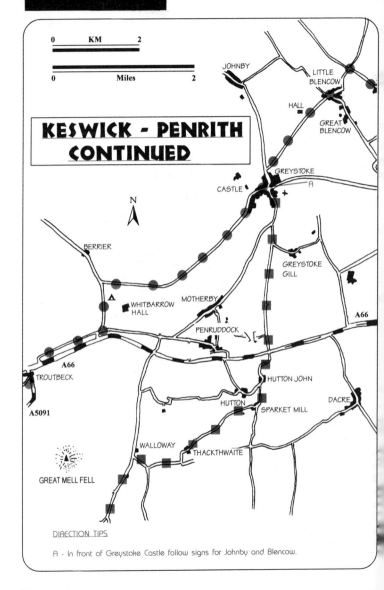

KESWICK - PENRITH CONTINUED

0 ___ KM ___ 2

0 ___ Miles ___ 2

N

JOHNBY

LITTLE BLENCOW

HALL

GREAT BLENCOW

GREYSTOKE

CASTLE

A

BERRIER

GREYSTOKE GILL

WHITBARROW HALL

MOTHERBY

PENRUDDOCK

A66

A66

TROUTBECK

HUTTON JOHN

DACRE

A5091

HUTTON

SPARKET MILL

WALLOWAY

THACKTHWAITE

GREAT MELL FELL

DIRECTION TIPS

A - In front of Greystoke Castle follow signs for Johnby and Blencow.

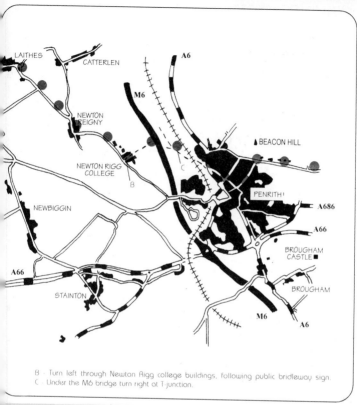

B - Turn left through Newton Rigg college buildings, following public bridleway sign.
C - Under the M6 bridge turn right at T-junction.

OTHER INFORMATION - PENRITH

Tourist Information Robinson's School, Middlegate (01768) 867466
Market Days Tues and Sat
Early Closing Wed
Hospital Penrith New Hospital, Bridge Lane (01768) 245300
Banks All the following have cashpoints: Barclays, Market Sq. Lloyds, 5-6 King St.
Midland, Market Sq. Natwest, 24-25 Devonshire St.
Cyle Shops Aragons, 2 Brunswick Rd (01768) 890344. Harpers, 1-2 Middlegate
(01768) 864475

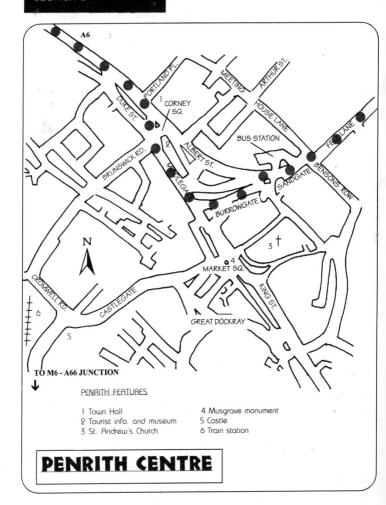

PENRITH FEATURES

1 Town Hall
2 Tourist info. and museum
3 St. Andrew's Church
4 Musgrave monument
5 Castle
6 Train station

PENRITH CENTRE

3 PENRITH - NENTHEAD

Section Distance 27 miles / 44km   **Off-road** 5 miles / 8 km

Accumulated Distance From Whitehaven 82 miles / 132km
From Workington 71 miles / 114km

The Route Leaving the gentle Eden Valley behind, you soon climb steeply to the spectacular viewpoint of Hartside before beginning the traverse of the Northern Pennines, 'England's Last Wilderness', much of it designated an Area of Outstanding Natural Beauty. Though lacking the alpine quality of the lakes the sombre, wide open spaces present, if anything, a more powerful landscape and there are certainly fewer settlements and chances for refreshment. **You should be aware of potentially extreme weather conditions if crossing this part of the route November - April.**

PENRITH - NENTHEAD

● **Edenhall** was based around a grand aristocratic home, demolished in 1934, once home of the Musgraves. The route passes the impressive entrance lodge and the stables with clock tower. The church is beautifully sited away from the village.

● **Langwathby** Compactly centred around the village green. Shepherds Inn Meals 12-2 and 6.30-8.30 Snacks from under £5 Cask ales plus mild and bitter. Shepherds Inn at Melmerby has meals 12-2.30 & 6-9.45. On A686 off route.

● **Little Salkeld** Nice walk to Lacey's Caves. Water-powered mill produces organic flours. Shop and tearoom. (01768) 881523.

● **Long Meg and her Daughters** Impressive prehistoric stone circle with large megalith at the head. 60 stones of 360 ft diameter. The purpose is unsure but it has possible funerary connections. Little Meg is a smaller circle to the north with no public access.

● **Hartside** Superb 580m viewpoint after a very tough climb out of the Eden Valley. Cafe by viewpoint.

● The **North Pennines Area of Outstanding Natural Beauty** is entered after climbing Hartside. Looks and feels barren but harbours a unique blend of flora, fauna (e.g. alpine flowers and birds such as the Merlin) and industrial archaeology. Great northern rivers, the Tyne, Tees, Wear and Derwent rise here. Several hills are crossed but the area is in fact one massive block of ancient rock, covered mainly in peat, 40 by 36 miles.

● **Garrigill** Blacksmith's Forge and Waterfalls Walk are on the alternative road route leaving Garrigill (Thortergill). Phone forge before arriving out of season. Tearooms 10-5 except Mondays, April-Oct. (01434) 381936

● **Ashgill Force** A fifty foot waterfall near Garrigill you can stand behind. Access by footpath from route (see map).

PENRITH - NENTHEAD
GRADIENT DIFFICULTY - VERY TOUGH

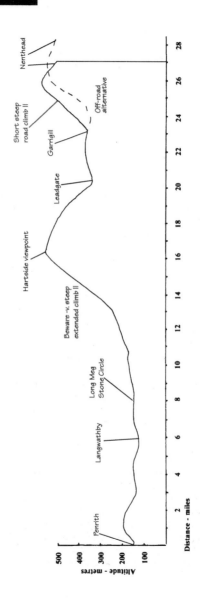

B&BS - Penrith to Garrigill

Langstanes, Culgaith Rd, Langwathby (01768) 881004 £££-PL-DR-LAU-SEC-WKSH. 200yds.
Langley House, Langwathby (01768) 881571 £££-PL-DR-LAU-SEC-WKSH. Near route.
Scalehouse Farm, Scalehouses nr Renwick (01768) 896493 ££-ME-PL-DR-LAU-SEC-WKSH. 2 miles
Horse and Jockey, Renwick (01768) 898579 ££-ME-PL-DR-LAU-SEC-WKSH. 1 mile.
Hill Top Cottage, Gamblesby (01768) 881069 £££-ME-PL-DR-LAU-SEC-WKSH. 1.5 miles
Half Way Bunkhouse, Busk, Renwick (01768) 898288 Camping barn-£-DR-SEC-Basic tools-Help yourself breakfast and self catering kitchen.
Brownside House, Leadgate (01434) 382169 ££-ME-PL-DR-LAU-SEC-Basic tools. 100yds.
Ivy House, Garrigill (01434) 382501 £££-PL-DR-LAU-SEC. Lots of extra facilities including pressure hose for washing, dinner and bike repair/hire.
The Post Office, Garrigill (01434) 381257 ££-PL-LAU-SEC-WKSH. 100yds.
High Windy Hall Hotel, above Garrigill on B6277. (01434) 381547 £25-£33-ME-PL-DR-SEC. Near route.
High Loaning Head Activity Centre, Garrigill (01434) 381929 Hostel type accommodation. ££-ME-PL-DR-LAU-SEC. Basic tools. Near route. Also stopover activities; canoes, lead mines, climbing etc.

ALSTON - HISTORY AND ATTRACTIONS

● Though not on the route **Alston** is frequently used by C2C riders as it's only a couple of miles off the route and has many facilities not available in Leadgate, Garrigil or Nenthead and is an attractive town. It lies at the junction of two 'A' roads and therefore you will have some relatively heavy traffic to face.
● Alston claims to be England's **highest market town** at 280m (919ft).
● Its greatest period of growth was based on a largely **Quaker-owned lead mining industry**. During its heyday in the nineteenth century the town had a population of 10,000 but is now down to 2,000. Tourism is now becoming one of the main industries.
● Many **old attractive buildings**, mainly nineteenth century. **Parish church** is one of the most notable, featuring the Derwentwater clock. Greenwich Hospital gained large estates in the area and gave the clock to the church.
● **South Tynedale Railway**. England's highest narrow gauge railway, running for 2.25 miles along former BR track. Next to the information centre and tea room housed in the old station. 40 minute trip through great scenery. Apr-Oct and Dec weekends (01434) 381696 Cont. on page 50

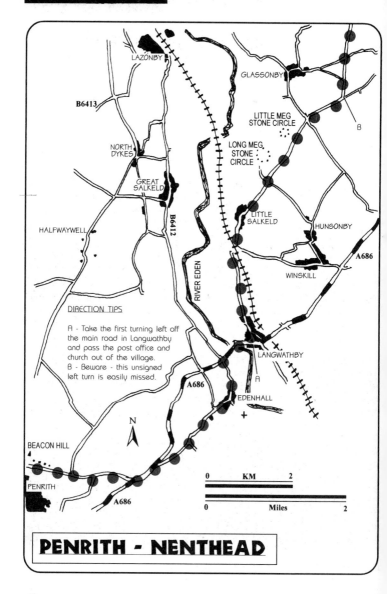

LAZONBY

GLASSONBY

B6413

LITTLE MEG
STONE CIRCLE

B

NORTH
DYKES

LONG MEG
STONE
CIRCLE

GREAT
SALKELD

B6412

LITTLE
SALKELD

HUNSONBY

HALFWAYWELL

A686

RIVER EDEN

WINSKILL

DIRECTION TIPS

A - Take the first turning left off
the main road in Langwathby
and pass the post office and
church out of the village.
B - Beware - this unsigned
left turn is easily missed.

LANGWATHBY

A686

A

EDENHALL

N

BEACON HILL

PENRITH

A686

0	KM	2

0	Miles	2

PENRITH - NENTHEAD

Long Meg and her Daughters in the Eden Valley

● **Important note on mining landscape:** The moorland landscape from the Alston area to the Waskerley Way is littered with remains of old mine workings. These include shafts, adits (horizontal tunnels for drainage or access) and old buildings such as smelt mills. **These are often in a serious state of decay and should not be entered.** As well as obvious sites such as vertical shafts beware of 'hummocky' ground which often contains pit entrances. 'Beehive' cones of stones covered pit entrances and may have partly collapsed. Some of these underground workings were hundreds of feet deep.

● The **Nent Force drainage level** began in Alston and was over four miles long when work ceased and took 60 years to build. Became a tourist attraction in the nineteenth century with boat trips and underground dancing! After extraction and smelting the lead was carried away by sturdy Galloway ponies.

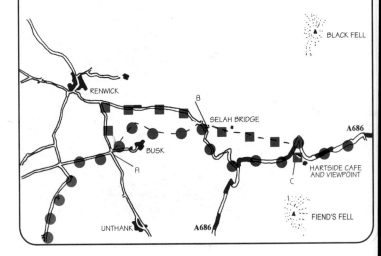

PENRITH - NENTHEAD CONTINUED

DIRECTION TIPS

A - For off-road option follow signed byway for Selah Bridge. For the road alternative turn left.
B - About 100m after the bridge take the bridleway track on the left signed Hartside. After passing a ruin the track soon becomes steep, and rocky. The road option is longer but easier!
C - Track short cut to Hartside cafe.

BLACK FELL

RENWICK

B

SELAH BRIDGE

A686

BUSK

A

HARTSIDE CAFE
AND VIEWPOINT
C

FIEND'S FELL

UNTHANK

A686

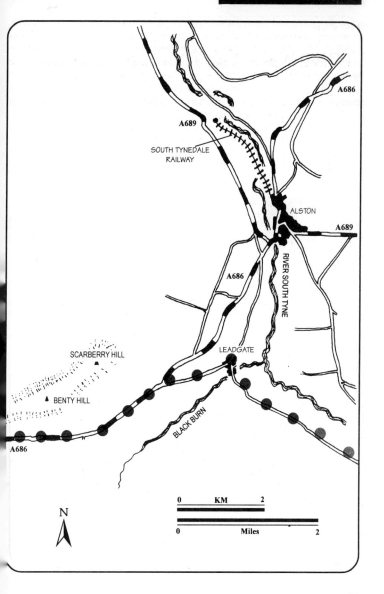

A686

A689

SOUTH TYNEDALE
RAILWAY

ALSTON

A689

A686

RIVER SOUTH TYNE

SCARBERRY HILL

▲ BENTY HILL

LEADGATE

BLACK BURN

A686

N

0	KM	2

0	Miles	2

PENRITH - NENTHEAD CONTINUED

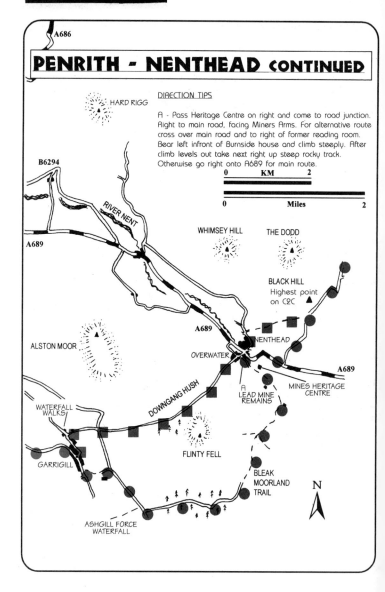

A686

HARD RIGG

DIRECTION TIPS

A - Pass Heritage Centre on right and come to road junction. Right to main road, facing Miners Arms. For alternative route cross over main road and to right of former reading room. Bear left infront of Burnside house and climb steeply. After climb levels out take next right up steep rocky track. Otherwise go right onto A689 for main route.

B6294

RIVER NENT

A689

WHIMSEY HILL

THE DODD

BLACK HILL
Highest point
on C2C

A689

ALSTON MOOR

NENTHEAD

OVERWATER

A689

MINES HERITAGE
CENTRE

DOWNGANG HUSH

A
LEAD MINE
REMAINS

WATERFALL
WALKS

GARRIGILL

FLINTY FELL

BLEAK
MOORLAND
TRAIL

N

ASHGILL FORCE
WATERFALL

ALSTON - ACCOMMODATION

Highfield, Bruntley Meadows (01434) 382182 ££-ME-PL-DR-LAU-SEC. 1.5 miles.

Alricia, 10 Bruntley Meadows (01434) 381307 ££-PL-DR-LAU-SEC. 1.5 miles.

Albert House Guest House, Townhead (01434) 381793 / (07887) 848790 £££-ME-PL-DR-LAU-SEC-WKSH. 1.5 miles.   Basic camping facilities also.

Cumberland Hotel, Townfoot (01434) 381875 £££-ME-PL-DR-LAU-SEC-WKSH. 1.5 miles. **Note:** Bunkhouse available from Christmas '97 £ Concessions at hotel and bunkhouse for C2C riders.

Blueberrys, Market Pl (01434) 381928 £££-ME-PL-DR-SEC. 1.5 miles. Restaurant attached. Open all day with range of meals up to £10.

Nentholme, The Butts (01434) 381523   ££££-ME-PL-DR-LAU-SEC-WKSH. 1.5 miles.

Chapel House (01434) 381112 ££-ME-PL-LAU-SEC-WKSH. 1.5 miles.

Lowber Manor Country House Hotel (01434) 381230   £££££-ME-PL-DR-SEC. 1.5 miles. Concessions for C2C riders.

Angel Inn, Front St (01434) 381363   ££-ME-PL-SEC. 1.5 miles.

Harbut Law, Brampton Rd (01434) 381950 £££-PL-DR-LAU-SEC-basic tools. 1.5 miles.

Alston Youth Hostel, The Firs (01434) 381509 £-ME-PL-DR-SEC. 1.5 miles

Alston Training and Adventure Centre, High Plains Lodge (01434) 381886. Hostel type accommodation from £ to £££-PL-DR-SEC-Basic repairs. Also ▲ On B6277 between Alston and Garrigill.

ALSTON - OTHER INFORMATION

Tourist Information The Railway Station (01434) 381696
Early Closing Tuesday
Hospital Ruth Lancaster James Lancaster Hospital (01434) 381218
Banks Barclays and Midland

NENTHEAD - HISTORY AND ATTRACTIONS

● Another **former mining settlement**. Less historic in appearance than Alston it still has features of interest, set amidst wild Pennine scenery. Claims to be England's highest village and has a climate to match (colder than Aberdeen). During winter travellers to Allendale found a journey through the mines easier than going 'over the tops'.

● Originally a **planned settlement for mine workers** (1825), organised by the same Quaker-based London Lead Company predominant in Alston. Enlightened attitude of the employers meant good working conditions for the time including provision of public baths and pension funds.

● **Reading room** and impressive **village hall** still remain. Well preserved **Methodist church** reflects former strength of religion.

● Interesting decorative **fountain** is a memorial to R.W. Bainbridge, superintendent of the mine company.

● Nenthead Mines **Heritage Centre and Historic Site**. Well-preserved site of 200 acres shows numerous remnants of lead and silver mining in its original forbidding landscape. New heritage centre tells the story of the site. Self-guided trails through the site plus Rampgill cafe. Plans to open up mines to the public in 1998. Admission charge. (01434) 382037

NENTHEAD - ACCOMMODATION

Cherry Tree, Nenthead (01434) 381434 ££-PL-DR-LAU-SEC-WKSH. Near route.
Mill Cottage Bunkhouse, Nenthead Mines (01434) 382037 £(££ with breakfast)-ME-PL-DR-LAU-SEC. On route.
Foulardrigg, Nenthead (01434) 382609 ££-PL-DR-LAU-SEC-WKSH. 0.75 miles.
Miners Arms, Nenthead (01434) 381427 ££ (B&B)-£ (Bunkhouse)-ME-PL-DR-LAU-SEC-Spares available. On route. Same establishment also has pub: Bkfst-8 onwards Lunch 12-2 Snacks 2-5 Evening meal 7-8.30. Real ales changed weekly. Boddingtons.
1 Glenview, Nenthead (01434) 381945 ££-ME-PL-DR-LAU-SEC-WKSH. Near route.

4 NENTHEAD - CONSETT

Section Distance 26 miles / 42km   **Off-road** 15 miles / 24km

Accumulated Distance From Whitehaven 108 miles / 174km
From Workington 97 miles / 156km

The Route You experience the highest point on the route during this section, Black Hill, at 609 metres (1998 ft), just beating Hartside. If anything the scenery of the North Pennines becomes wilder and grander and continues to be pockmarked by the remains of former mining activity. After climbing away from the extremely picturesque yet isolated Rookhope you can be secure in the knowledge that you have conquered the really mountainous part of the route and look forward to some downhill cruising to your final destination. The Waskerley Way is an excellent, level and largely well-surfaced dedicated cycle and walking trail that brings you to Consett. Lydgetts Junction has been chosen as the end point of this section as it is here you must make the choice of Newcastle or Sunderland as your finishing point.

NENTHEAD - CONSETT

● **County Durham** is entered soon after Allenheads. Known as 'Land of the Prince Bishops', the name reflects the historical power of these immensely powerful religio-military rulers. They were 'palatinate' rulers with powers equal to a king within their own territory. Such powerful figures were necessary to defend England's border from the Scottish threat.
● **Killhope Lead Mining Centre** About 5km off the route, east of Nenthead on A698. Underground visits down a mine and giant ore-grinding wheel amongst other attractions. April-October. Nov Sundays only. Admission charge. (01388) 537505
● **Allenheads** Despite a working history as a lead mining centre this is an estate village that has managed to reinvent itself as a small but popular tourist centre. Unlike lead mining in Nenthead the industry here was controlled largely by one aristocratic family, the Blackett-Beaumonts. Once a village of nearly 800 people it now has a population of around 200. The Allenheads mine closed in 1896, many workers emigrating to the colonies. (For individual attractions see pages 58-59).
● **Rookhope** Approaching Rookhope is a working fluorspar mine and further down the valley is the Lintzgarth arch, only remainder of a bridge that once carried a 2 mile long horizontal flue across the valley. This was cleaned by child labour to recoup lead deposits accumulated as smelting fumes were carried away up the hillside. An old smelt mill is in the centre. Main route over Stanhope Moor follows the line of an old railway line, once the highest standard gauge route in Britain, that carried mineral ore to Consett, continuing to the latter as the Waskerley Way. Rookhope Inn;

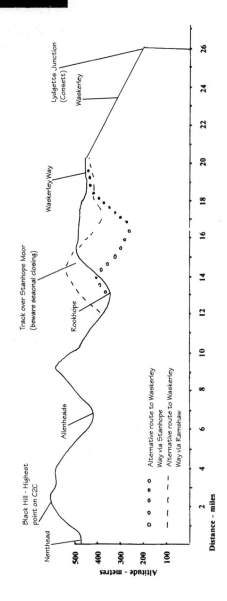

NENTHEAD - CONSETT
GRADIENT DIFFICULTY - VERY TOUGH

Black Hill - Highest point on C2C

Nenthead

Allenheads

Track over Stanhope Moor (beware seasonal closing)

Rookhope

Waskerley Way

Lydgetts Junction (Consett)

Waskerley

o o o o o   Alternative route to Waskerley Way via Stanhope
– – – –   Alternative route to Waskerley Way via Ramshaw

Altitude - metres

500 400 300 200 100

Distance - miles

2 4 6 8 10 12 14 16 18 20 22 24 26

56

Meals 12-2 Sat and Sun only, 7-9 Thurs-Mon (Tues -Weds by prior arrangement- see telephone below) £5 and up. Hadrian Gladiator, Hexamshire Devil's Water (free house with various guests). Information at Rookhope Nurseries.

B&Bs - Nenthead to Consett

Alston & Killhope Riding Centre, Low Cornriggs Farm, Cowshill (01388) 537600 £££(£)-ME-PL-DR-LAU-SEC. 3 miles.
Allenheads Lodge Outdoor Centre, Allenheads (01434) 685374 ££(£)-ME-PL-DR-LAU-SEC. Basic tools.
Spring House, Allenheads (01434) 685301 £££-ME-PL-DR-LAU-SEC-WKSH. Near route.
7 Front St. Rookhope (01388) 517577 £££-PL-DR-LAU-SEC-WKSH. Near route.
Rookhope Inn, Rookhope (01388) 517215 £££-ME-DR-PL-SEC. On route. See pub entry above. Also basic camping facilities.
Battsburn House, Rookhope (01388) 517414 ££-PL-DR-SEC-WKSH. Near route.

ALTERNATIVE ROUTE 1 - VIA RAMSHAW (16km)

● The more arduous but more **wildly picturesque** option. No services in Townfield or Ramshaw but Blanchland is about 3km off the route, north of Townfield.
● **Blanchland** A village created largely by aristocrats and known as one of the prettiest in Britain. Once based round a twelfth century abbey it fell into disrepair after the Dissolution but was beautifully restored and rebuilt by the Crewe family in the 18th century to house local lead miners. Lord Crewe Arms Hotel Meals 12-2.30 (2.00 Sundays) and 7-9 (9.15 Sundays)

ALTERNATIVE ROUTE 2 - VIA STANHOPE (11km)

● **Stanhope** Former lead mining town, now local market town with pretty centre. Recognised as the 'capital' of Weardale. Stanhope Castle is now converted to flats. Parish church of St. Thomas with fossilised tree stump and Roman altar to Silvanus (woodland god). Seventeenth century Stanhope Old Hall to the west of town. **Durham Dales Centre** Information, tea room and craft shop (01388) 527650 🚲 Weardale Mountain Bikes, Frosterley, Nr. Stanhope (01388) 528129

Stanhope B&Bs

Stanhope Old Hall Hotel and Restaurant, (01388) 528451 Prices from £35.00. Ask for C2C discount. ME-PL-DR-LAU-SEC-WKSH. Near route.
Red Lodge Guest House, Market Place (01388) 527851 £££-PL-DR-SEC.
Pack Horse Inn, 8 Market Place (01388) 528407. £££-ME-LAU-SEC.
Fairfield House, (01388) 528651 ££££-ME-PL-DR-LAU-SEC. Near route.

AROUND ALLENHEADS VILLAGE

1 Blacksmith's Shop and Offices Restored building with original blacksmith's tools. A museum collection of local artifacts has also been started.

2 Allenheads Inn Former 18th century residence of the aristocrat who inherited the local mines. Weather vane on roof shows his title, initials and date of accession.

3 Armstrong Engine House Contains 19th century hydraulic engine used for mine duties and a 20th century turbine which provided power to Allenheads Hall.

4 Hemmel Cafe Home baked food.

5 Heritage Centre Former 17th century inn. Now combines post office, shop and community centre with an exhibition on the history of the village. Closed Mondays and Fridays. April-Oct. Adjacent holiday cottage (01434) 685395

6 Family Nature Trail

7 Beaumont Hall Former mine offices, surrounded by estate workers and miners' cottages.

8 Allenheads Hall

Cottages at Allenheads

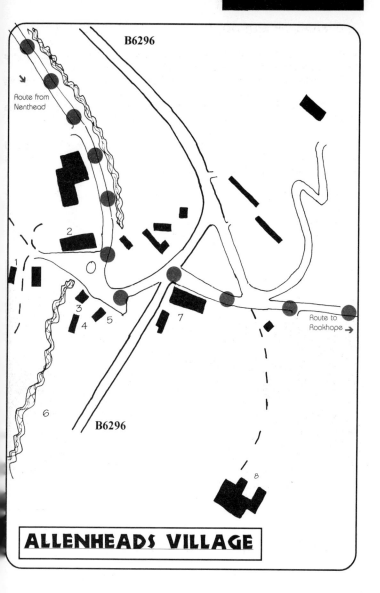

B6296

Route from
Nenthead

B6296

Route to
Rookhope →

ALLENHEADS VILLAGE

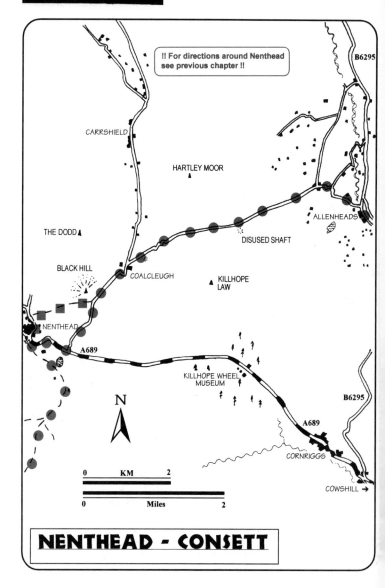

!! For directions around Nenthead
see previous chapter !!

B6295

CARRSHIELD

HARTLEY MOOR

ALLENHEADS

THE DODD

DISUSED SHAFT

BLACK HILL

COALCLEUGH

KILLHOPE
LAW

NENTHEAD

A689

KILLHOPE WHEEL
MUSEUM

B6295

N

A689

CORNRIGGS

COWSHILL →

| 0 | KM | 2 |

| 0 | Miles | 2 |

NENTHEAD - CONSETT

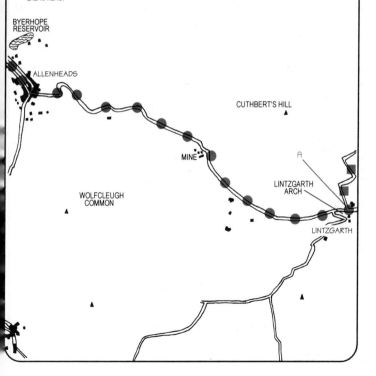

DIRECTION TIPS

A - First alternative route avoiding Stanhope Common track is this wild and lonely road through Townfield and Ramshaw. Go left at this junction, shortly after Lintzgarth Arch, signed for Blanchland.

BYERHOPE
RESERVOIR

ALLENHEADS

CUTHBERT'S HILL

MINE

A

LINTZGARTH
ARCH

WOLFCLEUGH
COMMON

LINTZGARTH

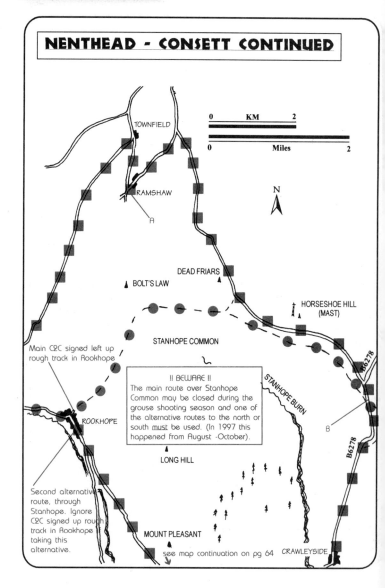

NENTHEAD - CONSETT CONTINUED

TOWNFIELD

RAMSHAW

A

KM

Miles

N

DEAD FRIARS

BOLT'S LAW

HORSESHOE HILL
(MAST)

Main C2C signed left up
rough track in Rookhope

STANHOPE COMMON

!! BEWARE !!
The main route over Stanhope
Common may be closed during the
grouse shooting season and one of
the alternative routes to the north or
south must be used. (In 1997 this
happened from August -October).

STANHOPE BURN

ROOKHOPE

B6278

B

LONG HILL

Second alternative
route, through
Stanhope. Ignore
C2C signed up rough
track in Rookhope
taking this
alternative.

B6278

MOUNT PLEASANT

see map continuation on pg 64

CRAWLEYSIDE

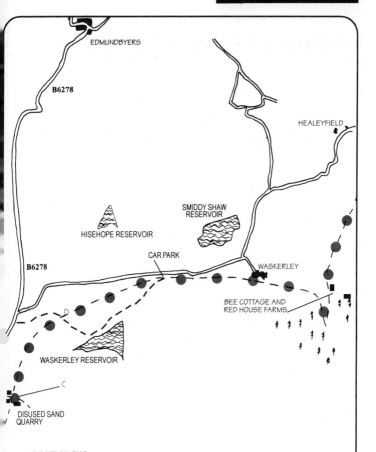

EDMUNDBYERS

B6278

HEALEYFIELD

SMIDDY SHAW
RESERVOIR

HISEHOPE RESERVOIR

CAR PARK

B6278

WASKERLEY

BEE COTTAGE AND
RED HOUSE FARMS

D

WASKERLEY RESERVOIR

C

DISUSED SAND
QUARRY

DIRECTION TIPS

A - Left before the no through road in Ramshaw, signed Stanhope / Blanchland.

B - The track across Stanhope Moor joins the B6278 along the top of an embankment. Bear right onto the road then immediate left up a track towards the disused corrugated metal quarry buildings.

C - At the track junction in the middle of the quarry buildings bear left and into open moorland again. Waskerley Reservoir appears down to your right.

D - Continue across this track crossroads.

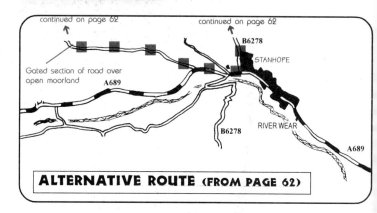

continued on page 62   continued on page 62

B6278

STANHOPE

Gated section of road over
open moorland   A689

B6278

RIVER WEAR

A689

ALTERNATIVE ROUTE (FROM PAGE 62)

AROUND CONSETT

● **Castleside** The Fleece Lunch 12-2 Evening Meals 6-9. Up to £5. S&N, Theakstons. ▲ Manor Caravan Park, Castleside (01207) 501000 5PL-WC-SH-DR April - Oct.

● **Consett** Previous centre of steel production, the town now suffers the economic effects of the dismantling of the massive site in 1980. Steel was the main source of income and the works stretched for over a mile. ⬦ Consett Bicycle Co. 62-4 Medomsley Rd. (01207) 581205

B&Bs - Around Consett

Castleneuk Guest House, 18-20 Front Street, Castleside (01207) 506634 £££-ME-PL-DR-SEC. Some tools.

Bee Cottage Farm, Castleside (01207) 508224 ££££-ME-PL-LAU-SEC. Near route and signed from it.

Consett YMCA, Parliament St, Consett (01207) 502680 ££-ME-PL-DR-LAU-SEC. Near route.

C2C SIGNS

Right: Old style C2C sign beneath a Waterside trail sign, near Tynemouth (section 5B). Old style signs are being replaced with new signs bearing the number 7.
Below: Look out for C2C stencils on the road or path surface such as this one at Consett.

C2C ARCHITECTURE

Left: Moot Hall, Keswick
(section 2)
Below: The beautiful Tourist
Information Office in
Cockermouth (section 1B)

Right: Memorial fountain in
Nenthead (section 3)
Below: Cottages at Allenheads
(section 4)

Above: Gibside Chapel near Rowland's Gill (section 5B)
Below: Ruined hall, also on Gibside estate

C2C TRACKS AND PATHS

Above: Keswick Railway Path (section 2)
Left: Moorland track, coming into Nenthead (section 3)
Previous Page: Whitehaven to Ennerdale Railway Path (section 1A)

C2C SCULPTURE
Above: Whitehaven - Ennerdale Path (section 1A)
Below: 'Phoenix' bridge on Whitehaven - Ennerdale Path (section 1A)
Overleaf: 'King Cole', Consett - Sunderland Path (section 5A)

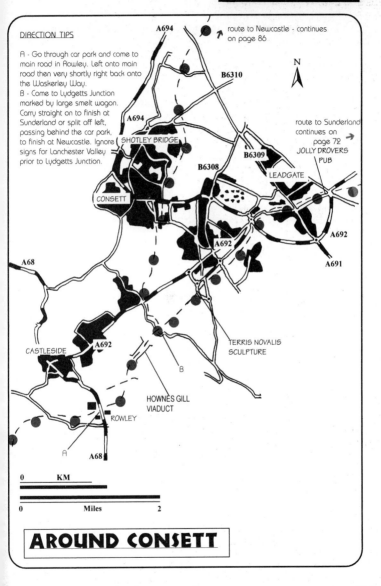

route to Newcastle - continues on page 86

DIRECTION TIPS

A - Go through car park and come to main road in Rowley. Left onto main road then very shortly right back onto the Waskerley Way.

B - Come to Lydgetts Junction marked by large smelt wagon. Carry straight on to finish at Sunderland or split off left, passing behind the car park, to finish at Newcastle. Ignore signs for Lanchester Valley prior to Lydgetts Junction.

A694

A694

B6310

B6308

B6309

SHOTLEY BRIDGE

CONSETT

LEADGATE

route to Sunderland continues on page 72
JOLLY DROVERS PUB

A692

A692

A691

A68

A692

TERRIS NOVALIS SCULPTURE

CASTLESIDE

B

HOWNES GILL VIADUCT

ROWLEY

A

A68

0   KM

0   Miles   2

AROUND CONSETT

65

5A CONSETT - SUNDERLAND (OPTION)

Section Distance 25 miles / 40km

Off-road Virtually all off-road with occasional road section

Accumulated Distance From Whitehaven 133miles / 214km
From Workington 122 miles / 196km

The Route For most of the way the Consett and Sunderland railway path is flat and easy to follow. The real difficulties in navigation lie in negotiating Sunderland city centre (not as difficult as Newcastle). Physically, however, this is the easiest section of the whole route. The landscape presents a strong contrast; the Wear Valley is delightfully green and wooded in places, dotted with specially commissioned sculptures and other monuments, whilst Sunderland presents a grand spectacle of post-industrial decay that is steadily and thoughtfully being regenerated, together with many interesting museums and buildings.

STANLEY TO WASHINGTON

- Worked for centuries as an industrial site, much of the landscape passed through has been designated as the **Great North Forest**, a current environmental initiative to re-green a wide area with forest or hedgerow, and make it a pleasant place for relaxation and recreation.
- **Stanley** Former coal mining settlement now houses Sustrans' North Eastern Office (Rockwood House, Barn Hill [01207] 281259). General information and C2C T-shirt. See the comments of other C2C riders in their visitors book! Callers welcome.
- **Causey Arch** To the north of Stanley, now a Scheduled Ancient Monument. Built in 1727 as part of Tanfield Waggonway to carry coal. 105ft long and 80ft high at the centre of picnic and recreation area. Horses pulled the coal along the wooden rails. Local designer of bridge used Roman model for its single-span construction.
- **Tanfield Railway** World's oldest existing railway. Volunteer-manned, running alongside the arch where it stops. Station, engine shed and workshops at Marley Hill. Trains run throughout the year between Sunniside, Causey Arch and East Tanfield. Admission charge. Talking timetable (0191) 2742002
  - ⚲ Roy Duncan Mountain Bike Hire, 1 West Hills, Tantobie (north west of Stanley) (01207) 237010
- **Beamish Open Air Museum** A unique full-scale recreation of the past industrial and agricultural life of the North-East. Visit a drift mine, pit cottages, a 19th century manor farm or hop on a tram, plus lots more attractions at this huge site in Beamish Burn. Also houses a tourist information centre. Admission fee. (01207) 231811.
  - ⚲ Cycle Hire available from Sustrans at Beamish.

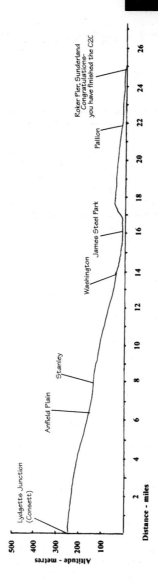

CONSETT - SUNDERLAND
GRADIENT DIFFICULTY - EASY

Looking north from the Waskerley Way near Waskerley (section 4)

△ **Bobby Shafto Caravan Park**, Cranberry Plantation, Beamish (0191) 3701776 WC-SH-SHP March - Oct.

● **Chester-le-Street** Few physical remains left of Roman influence in its name but impressive spire on church and effigies of the Lumley family inside. **Ankers House Museum**, Church Chare, town centre. See how an Anchorite lived, walled up for life to pray! Free admission (0191) 3883295. April-Oct, Mon-Sat

● **James Steel Park** surrounds the Wear between Fatfield and Barmston. Houses Victoria Viaduct (completed on Victoria's coronation day, 28th June, 1838) and Worm Hill of Lambton Worm fame. The 'Worm' was a mythical dragon that brought about a family curse when slain.

● **The Penshaw Monument** is based on the Temple of Hephaestus in Athens. A memorial to 'Radical Jack' Lambton, 1st Earl of Durham, it was built in 1844 from public subscription. Good views of it from James Steel Park and around Cox Green.

● **Washington Wildfowl Trust** Important and extensive site for wildlife, especially winter wildfowl. Admission charge. (0191) 4165454

● **Washington** Created as a new town in 1967, it was designed to attract industry and jobs to a declining area. Divided into self-contained village type settlements and with planned segregation of cars and pedestrians. **Washington Old Hall**, The Avenue, District 4, Washington Village. A National Trust property incorporating the remains of the home of George Washington's ancestors, within a 17th century manor house. (0191) 4166879 for opening details. **'F' Pit Mining Museum**, Albany Way. Winding house and engine on display. **Washington Arts Centre**, Fatfield, houses exhibitions and performances.

B&Bs - Stanley to Washington

Tanfield Lane Farm, Tanfield nr Stanley (01207) 232739 £££-PL-LAU-SEC-Basic tools. 1 mile.

Oak Tree Inn, Tantobie (NW of Stanley) (01207) 235445 ££££-ME-PL-DR-LAU-SEC. 0.5 miles.

No Place House, Beamish (0191) 3700891 / (0378) 150422 £££-DR-LAU-SEC. Basic tools. 0.5 miles.

Beamish Mary Inn, No Place, Beamish (0191) 3700237 ££££-PL-LAU-SEC. 600m from route. Also a pub: Meals 12-2.30 and 7-9.30. Up to £10.00. Real ales and guest beers.

Malling Guest House, Oakdale Terrace, Newfield (nr. Beamish) (0191) 3702571 £££(£)-ME-PL-DR-LAU-SEC-WKSH. 0.3 miles.

Waldridge Fell Guest House, Waldridge, Chester-le Street (0191) 3891908 ££££(£)-SEC. 3 miles

The Village farmhouse, Village Lane, Washington (0191) 4153355 ££££-PL-DR-LAU-SEC

SUNDERLAND - HISTORY AND ATTRACTIONS

● Once one of the world's greatest **shipbuilding** towns. The shipbuilding area can still be seen from Wearmouth Bridge. One of England's **newest cities** and the centre of much regeneration, e.g. St. Peter's Riverside development; after June 1998 this area will house the **National Glass Centre**. Wearmouth also houses the **'Stadium of Light'** football ground, new for the 97-8 season and the C2C passes a new marina development. For **Wear ferries** contact Tourist Information (pg70)

● **Wearmouth Bridge** road bridge dwarfs the railway bridge next to it. Built 1927-8. The parapet has a medallion showing the 1796 bridge it replaced.

● **North East Aircraft Museum**. 3 miles west of Sunderland off the A1290. Collection of aircraft, aero-engines and military vehicles. Admission charge. Tel (0191) 5813602 Restricted opening October-May.

● **St. Andrew's Church**, Roker. The 'cathedral' of William Morris' Arts and Craft Movement.

● **Fulwell Mill**. North of Roker. Most complete windmill in the north east. Restored. For location of following attractions see map on pages 74-75.

● **Hylton Castle**. 15th century keep-gatehouse still survives. West side has heavy battlements. Good display of medieval heraldry. Admission charge. (0191) 5480152

● **St.Peters Church**. One of Northumbria's oldest churches with Saxon wall and tower. Home of the Venerable Bede, 'Father of English History'. Much of it reconstructed in Victorian times. Easter-Oct, weekdays 2- 4.30. (0191)-5673726

● **Monkwearmouth Land Transport Museum**. Housed in train station with grand classical facade. Railway museum with a genuine 19th century atmosphere. Free admission. (0191) 5677075

● **Sunderland Museum and Art Gallery**. Shipbuilding, wildlife and the Sunderland story. (0191) 5650723

● **Sunderland Volunteer Life Brigade Museum**. Near the end of the C2C. Volunteers preceded the RNLI as the main body responsible on this stretch of coast for ship rescue. Originally used the 'breeches buoy' method of rescue. Brigade now separated from the coastguard service and act as auxiliary service for coastal services and cliff rescue. Still a working brigade; only one of 3 left out of an original 40. Free entry. Sunday 12-6 and some evenings. (0191) 5672579

● **National Glass Centre** Major new development next to the route housing incredible glass sculpture, gallery exhibitions, shop and restaurant. Open daily. (0191) 5155555

SUNDERLAND - ACCOMMODATION

Brendon House, 49 Roker Park Road, Roker (0191) 5489303 ££-ME-PL-DR-LAU-SEC-WKSH. 0.25 miles.

Belmont Guest House, 8 St. Georges Ter. Roker (0191) 5672438 ££-ME-PL-DR-LAU-SEC. Near route.

Ashborne Guest House, 7 St. Georges Ter. Roker (0191) 5653997 £££-ME-PL-DR-LAU-SEC. Near route.

Park Avenue Hotel, Southclife, Roker (0191) 5653011 £££(£)-ME-PL-DR-LAU-SEC.

Chaise and Balmoral Guest Houses, 3 &5 Roker Ter (0191) 5659218 / 5659217 ££-ME-PL-DR-LAU-SEC. Near route.

Beach View Guest House, 15 Roker Ter (0191) 5670719 £££-SEC. Near route.

April Guest House, 12 St. Georges Ter. Roker (0191) 5659550 £££-DR-SEC. Near route.

Anchor Lodge Guest House, 16 Roker Ter. (0191) 5674154 ££-ME-PL-DR-LAU-SEC-Basic tools. Near route.

SUNDERLAND - OTHER INFORMATION

Tourist Information Fawcett St. (0191) 553 2000/2001/2002
Market days Jacky White's Market and Park Lane Market; Mon-Sat
Early Closing Wednesday
Hospital Sunderland District General Hospital, Kayll Rd (0191) 5656256
Banks All the following have cashpoints. Barclays, 53 Fawcett St. Lloyds, 54 Fawcett St. Midland, 14 Fawcett St. Natwest, 52 Fawcett St.
Cycle Shops Darke Cycles, 113 High St West (0191) 5108155. Cycle World, 118 High St. West (0191) 5658188. The Big Bike Shop, 212 High St West (0191) 5679090

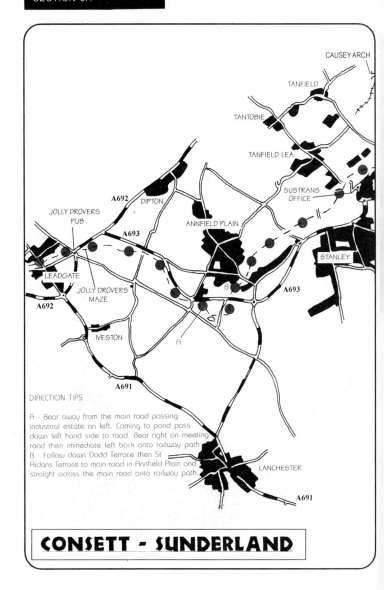

CAUSEY ARCH

TANFIELD

TANTOBIE

TANFIELD LEA

SUSTRANS OFFICE

A692   DIPTON

JOLLY DROVERS PUB

ANNFIELD PLAIN

A693

STANLEY

LEADGATE

JOLLY DROVERS MAZE

A692

B

A693

IVESTON

A

A691

DIRECTION TIPS

A - Bear away from the main road passing industrial estate on left. Coming to pond pass down left hand side to road. Bear right on meeting road then immediate left back onto railway path
B - Follow down Dodd Terrace then St Aidans Terrace to main road in Annfield Plain and straight across the main road onto railway path.

LANCHESTER

A691

CONSETT - SUNDERLAND

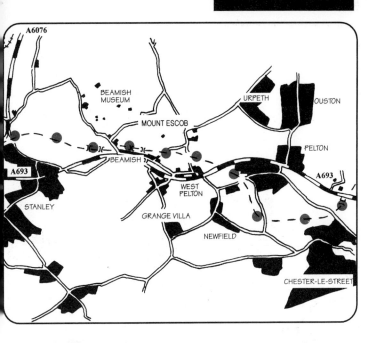

A6076

BEAMISH
MUSEUM

URPETH

OUSTON

MOUNT ESCOB

PELTON

BEAMISH

A693

WEST
PELTON

A693

STANLEY

GRANGE VILLA

NEWFIELD

CHESTER-LE-STREET

Entrance to Beamish Museum

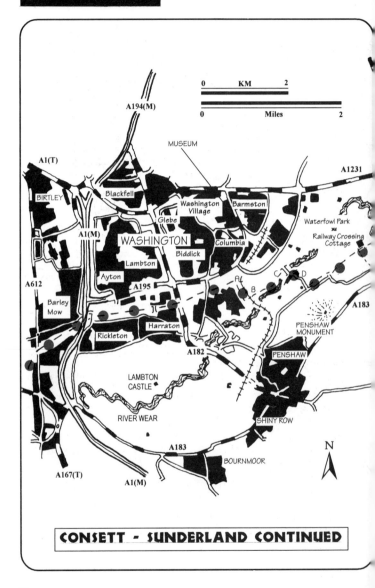

0 KM 2

0 Miles 2

A194(M)

MUSEUM

A1(T)

A1231

BIRTLEY

Blackfell

Washington
Village

Barmston

Glebe

Waterfowl Park

A1(M)

WASHINGTON

Columbia

Railway Crossing
Cottage

Biddick

A612

Lambton

A

Ayton

A195

B

C D

A183

Barley
Mow

PENSHAW
MONUMENT

Rickleton

Harraton

PENSHAW

A182

LAMBTON
CASTLE

RIVER WEAR

SHINY ROW

N

A183

A167(T)

A1(M)

BOURNMOOR

CONSETT - SUNDERLAND CONTINUED

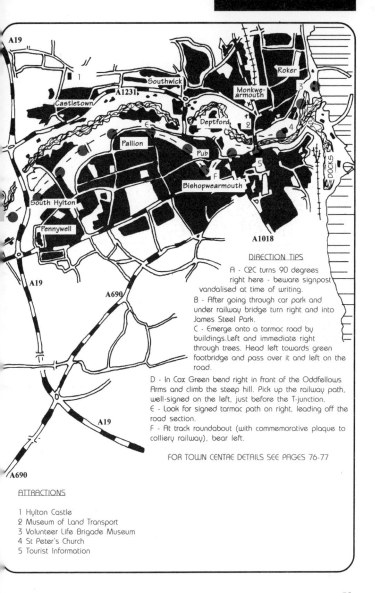

DIRECTION TIPS

A - C2C turns 90 degrees right here - beware signpost vandalised at time of writing.

B - After going through car park and under railway bridge turn right and into James Steel Park.

C - Emerge onto a tarmac road by buildings. Left and immediate right through trees. Head left towards green footbridge and pass over it and left on the road.

D - In Cox Green bend right in front of the Oddfellows Arms and climb the steep hill. Pick up the railway path, well-signed on the left, just before the T-junction.

E - Look for signed tarmac path on right, leading off the road section.

F - At track roundabout (with commemorative plaque to colliery railway), bear left.

FOR TOWN CENTRE DETAILS SEE PAGES 76-77

ATTRACTIONS

1 Hylton Castle
2 Museum of Land Transport
3 Volunteer Life Brigade Museum
4 St Peter's Church
5 Tourist Information

C2C THROUGH SUNDERLAND CENTRE

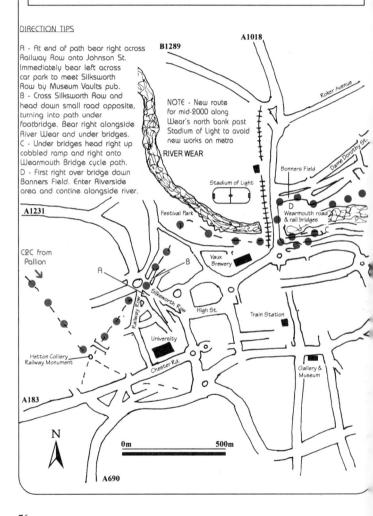

DIRECTION TIPS

A - At end of path bear right across Railway Row onto Johnson St. Immediately bear left across car park to meet Silksworth Row by Museum Vaults pub.
B - Cross Silksworth Row and head down small road opposite, turning into path under footbridge. Bear right alongside River Wear and under bridges.
C - Under bridges head right up cobbled ramp and right onto Wearmouth Bridge cycle path.
D - First right over bridge down Bonners Field. Enter Riverside area and contine alongside river.

NOTE - New route for mid-2000 along Wear's north bank past Stadium of Light to avoid new works on metro

RIVER WEAR

A1018
B1289
Roker Avenue
Dame Dorothy St.
Bonners Field
Stadium of Light
D
Wearmouth road & rail bridges
A1231
Festival Park
C2C from Pallion
A
B
Silksworth Row
High St.
Vaux Brewery
Train Station
University
Hetton Colliery Railway Monument
Chester Rd.
Gallery & Museum
A183
Railway Row
N
0m   500m
A690

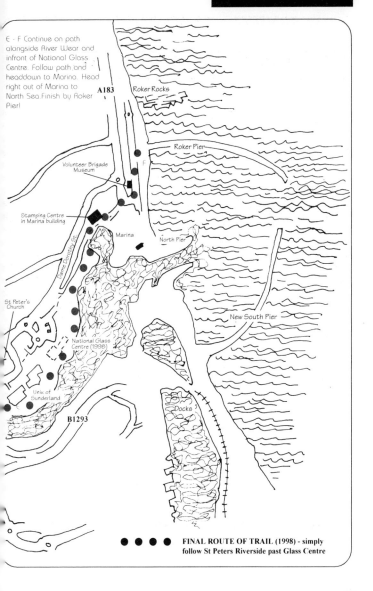

E - F Continue on path alongside River Wear and infront of National Glass Centre. Follow path and headdown to Marina. Head right out of Marina to North Sea.Finish by Roker Pier!

A183

Roker Rocks

Roker Pier

Volunteer Brigade Museum

F

Stamping Centre in Marina building

Marina

North Pier

Dame Dorothy St

St Peter's Church

National Glass Centre (1998)

New South Pier

Univ. of Sunderland

B1293

Docks

● ● ● ● **FINAL ROUTE OF TRAIL (1998) - simply follow St Peters Riverside past Glass Centre**

5B CONSETT - TYNEMOUTH (OPTION)

Section Distance 31 miles / 50km   **Off-road** 20 miles / 32km

Accumulated Distance From Whitehaven 139 miles / 223.5km
From Workington 128 miles / 206km

The Route Gentle downhill pedalling, with lengthy sections on specially surfaced off-road track on various designated trails. The Derwent Walk is followed for much of its length from Consett to Swalwell. There is then a 'messy' alternative option along the Tyne's southern bank, following the Keelman's Way to the Tyne Bridge rejoining the main route here to continue on the Keelmans Way to Hebburn. The main route along the northern bank to the swing bridge is recommended (easier to navigate and more scenic). From the swing bridge the Keelman's Way is followed to the Tyne Pedestrian Tunnel and then parts of the Waterside Trail and sections of minor road lead to your ultimate destination on the C2C, the north pier at Tynemouth. Although the route is significantly longer than the Sunderland option there are few more dramatic sights on the route than Newcastle's skyline next to the series of bridges culminating in the famous Tyne Bridge. The forested scenery of the Derwent Walk equals the more pastoral sections of the approach to Sunderland, but both cities ,of course, have their 'rough edges'. The major difficulty in several sections on the Newcastle option is navigation. Be prepared for careful use of maps and attention to the direction tips, as the route twists and turns its way along the Tyne's banks. Navigation will hopefully be easier from mid-1998 when the route is planned to follow Hadrian's Wall National Trail along the north bank, from the swing bridge to the Tyne Tunnel exit.

CONSETT TO THE RIVER TYNE

● Much of the route from Consett to the Tyne follows the lovely **Derwent Walk Path**, based on the line of the 19th century Derwent Valley Railway which carried passengers and goods between the two. It crosses spectacular viaducts such as Pontburn, Fogoesburn and Nine Arches. Now tree-clad along much of its length and housing wildlife such as woodpeckers and sparrowhawks. Largest area of ancient woodland is around Thornley Woodland Centre. Derwent Walk Country Park surrounding the path is one of the largest in northern England.

● Approaching Consett the rough area of wasteland is **Berry Edge**, 700 acre site of the former Consett steelworks, closed in 1980.

● **Shotley Bridge** Home of 17th century swordmakers, this spa town still houses reminders of this era such as the Cutlers Hall. Crown and Crossed Swords Pub, Front St . Breakfast , lunch and evening meals daily. Also Manor House Inn (see B&B section).

● **Ebchester** Site of the Roman fort Vindamora. Small museum at Mains Farm includes hypocaust (heated space under the floor of a Roman house). The site was once on Dere Street, the Roman road bringing supplies north, connecting York and the Firth of Forth. Opposite church in Ebchester village. Viewed by appointment (01207) 562180. Derwent Walk Pub Meals 12-4 and 6-9.30. £5-10. Jennings and other real ales. ▲ Byreside Caravan Site, Hamsterley (01207) 560280 WC-SHP

● **Rowlands Gill** Developed as a mining settlement this is now a pleasant residential suburb with numerous shops and pub. ▲ Derwent Park Caravan and Camping Site WC-SH. April 1st-September 30th. (01207) 543383

● **Gibside** Beautiful 18th century landscaped grounds including Old Hall, extraordinary Palladian Chapel, Orangery, British Liberty statue and Banqueting Hall. Allow a couple of hours to stroll round grounds. Coal-owner George Bowes was responsible for most of the magnificent relandscaping and is buried in the chapel crypt. National Trust. Admission charge. Opening details ring (01207) 542255. A real 'must'. See direction tip 'D', page 87.

B&Bs - CONSETT - RIVER TYNE

Manor House Inn, Shotley Bridge (01207) 255268 £££(£)-PL-DR-SEC. 2-3km. Also a pub: Meals 12-2.30 and 7-9.30 (Sun 7-9 only).Beamish and guest ales.

NEWCASTLE UPON TYNE- HISTORY AND ATTRACTIONS

● Most famous for **heavy industry and coal**. Previously one of the largest ship building and repair centres in the world. The cranes and derricks around Walker Riverside are still an impressive spectacle and Swan Hunter are still active here.

● Once had one of the most **elegant townscapes** in the country and countless interesting buildings and monuments remain despite crass 60s and 70s modernisation (see map and key. Pgs 84-85). **Grey St**. has been described as one of the most elegant streets in Europe.

● Also famous for bridges, most notably the **Tyne Bridge**, suspended by the huge suspension arch. Bridges near city centre are, from west to east:

Redheugh Bridge (1900); Road bridge.

King Edward Bridge (1906); Railway bridge.

Queen Elizabeth II; Metro bridge.

High Level Bridge (1849); Railway, road and foot passengers. Designed by Robert Stephenson. One of the wonders of the Railway Age.

Hydraulic Swing Bridge (1876); Road bridge. One of the first large opening bridges in the world. It turns on a pivot whose centre is the small blue tower.

Tyne Bridge (1928); Road Bridge.

● The **Quayside** area of the centre has a famous Sunday morning open market.

Discovery Museum, Blandford Sq. Tells the history of Newcastle through a host of diverse galleries. Open Mon-Sat. (0191) 2326789

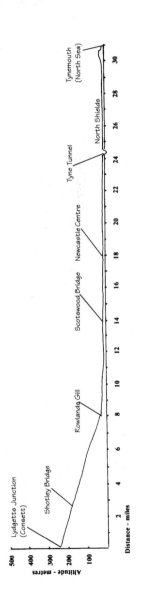

CONSETT - NEWCASTLE
GRADIENT DIFFICULTY - EASY

● **Military Vehicle Museum**, Exhibition Park. Open daily (0191) 2817222
● **Newburn Hall Motor Museum**, Townfield Gardens, Newburn. 5 miles west of centre along A695. Open Tues-Sun. (0191) 2642977.
●**Jesmond Dene**. Park in steep sided valley created by armaments manufacturer Baron Armstrong. To north east of city centre.

NEWCASTLE - ACCOMMODATION

The Grove Hotel, 134-138 Brighton Grove, Fenham, Newcastle (0191) 2738248 ££££-ME-PL-DR-LAU. Fenham is north of Elswick (north bank of Tyne). 2-3km.
The Brighton, 47 -51 Brighton Grove, Fenham (0191) 2733600 / 2260563 ££(£)-ME-PL-SEC. 2-3 km.
Corner House, Heaton Rd (0191) 2659602 £34.95 per room (whether double, single or family). ME-PL. Heaton is 3-4 km north east of Newcastle city centre, north of Byker.
Grosvenor House, Grosvenor Rd, Jesmond (0191) 2810543 ££££(£)-ME-DR-SEC. Jesmond is just to the west of Heaton, 3-4 km from the route.
Avenue Hotel, Osborne Avenue, Jesmond (0191) 2811396 £££££-ME-SEC.
Newcastle Youth Hostel, 107 Jesmond Rd. (0191) 2812570 £-ME-PL-SEC. 1.5 miles.

NEWCASTLE - OTHER INFORMATION

Tourist Information Central Library, Princess Sq. (0191) 2610610. Also at Central Station (0191) 2300030
Market Days Grainger Covered Market; Mon-Sat. Quayside Market; Sunday mornings. Bigg Market; Tues, Thurs, Sat.
Hospital Royal Victoria Infirmary, Royal Vivtoria Rd (0191) 2325131
Banks All the following have cashpoints. Barclays, Grainger St. - Lloyds, Grey St. Midland, 42 Grey St. Natwest, 16 Northumberland St.
Bike Shops The Bike Place, 8 Allison Court, Metro Centre (0191) 4883137. Newcastle Cycle Centre, 165 Westgate Rd. (0191) 2303022. Denton Cycles, 21 Blenheim St. (0191) 2323903 Cycle Logical, 37 St. Georges Terr. Jesmond (0191) 818383 Hardisty Cycles, 5 Union Rd. Byker (0191) 2658619 Lavericks Cycles, 22 Station Rd. Cullercoats, North Shields (0191) 2524491

NEWCASTLE - TYNEMOUTH

● From the confluence of the Derwent and the Tyne the Scotswood Bridge takes you onto the north bank. **Hadrian's Trail** is followed to the Swing Bridge. Along the way the riverside path passes through the old industrial area, with descriptive plaques. On the opposite bank the massive frame of **Dunston Staithes** comes into view. Used to load coal onto ships and claimed to be the largest wooden structure in the world.   (Maps 1 and 2)

● On the **southern bank** of the Tyne, after passing the swing bridge, the route passes opposite the traditional shipbuilding areas of **Byker** and **Walker** (the proposed route to open in 1998 will pass through them), following the Keelman's Way, before crossing the **Tyne Tunnel.** (Maps 3 to 6)

● **Royal Quays** An enormous shopping and housing redevelopment area. Look out for the viewpoint in Redburn Dene park. (Map 7)

● Passing through the quayside area of North Shields you come to **Tynemouth**. The two white towers above and on the quay are navigational aids that ships could use to navigate a safe passage up the Tyne (done by aligning them). **Clifford's Fort** near the Fish Quay is the remains of a seventeenth century armed fort named after Lord Clifford of Cabal. (Map 8)

● **Black Middens** Once notorious rocks near the Tyne entrance. Claimed 5 ships in 3 days in November 1864. (Map 8)

● **Collingwood Monument** This native of Newcastle took command of the fleet at Trafalgar and continues to look over the mouth of the Tyne today. (Map 8)

● **Tynemouth Priory and Castle**, surrounded by curiously eroded gravestones, overlooks your finishing point by the pier. Originally an 11th century Norman church and developed within a castle enclosure. Percy Chantry is the only complete part left (heavily restored). English Heritage site. April-Oct open daily Nov-March Weds to Sun. Coastguard's regional H.Q. lies alongside. (Map 8)

Tynemouth B&Bs

Northumberland Bothy, Tynemouth Station (01830) 540342 and (0191) 2583167 £(£) PL-DR-LAU. Bunk beds, showers, toilets and bike store. Bedding available. Stamping point. 20th March-30th Nov. Coffee shop opposite.

Also try: The 61, 61 Front St. (0191) 2573687 £££

There is also a branch of Barclays on Front St. with cashpoint.

ynemouth Priory and Castle remains near the C2C finish

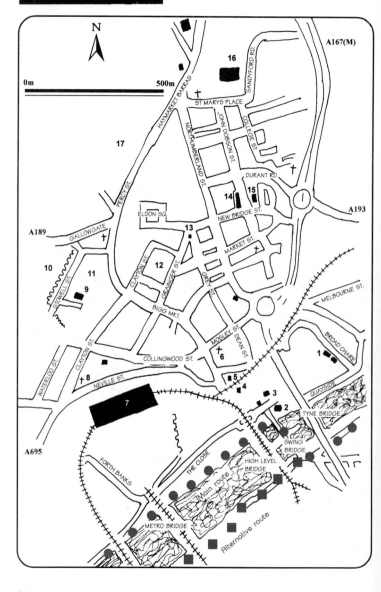

NEWCASTLE TOWN CENTRE MAP

1 TRINITY MARITIME CENTRE Restored ships' chandlers warehouses, including museum. (0191) 2614691

2 GUILDHALL Containing the magnificent Merchants' Court.

3 BESSIE SURTEES' HOUSE 17th century timber-framed building. Named after a lady who eloped from here. (0191) 2611585

4 CASTLE KEEP Part of the castle built between 1172 and 1178 by Henry II. The original castle gave its name to the city. The 82ft high tower with 18ft thick walls was subsequently used as a jail.

5 BLACK GATE Added to the castle in 1247. Guarded the only level approach to the castle. Passing through the gate is the Heron Pit, an underground prison.

6 ST. NICHOLAS' CATHEDRAL has a remarkably beautiful 15th century 'crown' spire. The only other in the UK in this style is in Edinburgh. Inside features are the Collingwood Monument and the brass lectern. Nearly destroyed by Scottish troops during the Civil War but the Mayor surrounded the tower with Scottish POWs to stop it being fired upon.

7 CENTRAL STATION Impressive creation of the Industrial Revolution with a classical facade and massive wrought iron and glass roof. Opened by Queen Victoria in 1850. Also houses useful TOURIST INFORMATION OFFICE.

8 ST. MARY'S CATHEDRAL 19th century, Gothic style. Designed by Pugin who helped in designing the Houses of Parliament.

9 BLACKFRIARS Remains of famous 13th century monastery. Monarchy usually resided whilst visiting Newcastle.

10 REMAINS OF CITY WALLS Built during the reigns of Edward I and Edward II. They were maintained until the Napoleonic Wars after which they fell into disuse so only sections remain, such as that here.

11 CHINATOWN Chinese district with many fine restaurants.

12 GRAINGER MARKET 19th century buildings continue as an indoor market.

13 GREY'S MONUMENT Commemorates 1832 Reform Act passed under Earl Grey's premiership. (For the first time the middle classes had the vote).

14 TOURIST INFORMATION (In the library building)

15 LAING ART GALLERY AND MUSEUM Paintings, silver, glass and costumes. Art on Tyneside.

16 CIVIC CENTRE Interesting 1960s building with notable Tyne God and Swans in Flight statues.

17 NEWCASTLE UNIVERSITY COMPLEX Houses numerous museums including Museum of Antiquities, Greek Museum, Hatton Gallery (art and African sculpture). Nearby museums also include Hancock Museum (stuffed fauna and geological gallery).

For attractions not on city centre map see 'Newcastle - History and Attractions', pages 79 and 81.

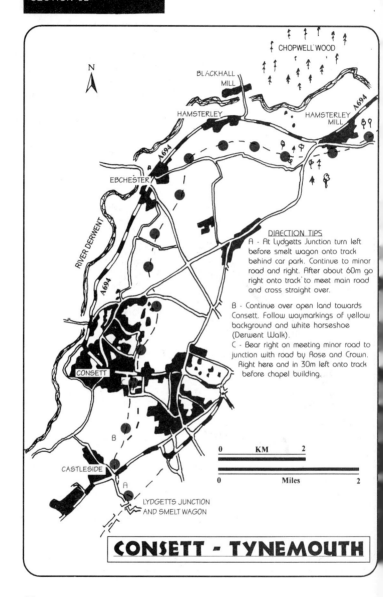

CHOPWELL WOOD

BLACKHALL MILL

HAMSTERLEY

HAMSTERLEY MILL

A694

EBCHESTER

RIVER DERWENT

A694

CONSETT

B

CASTLESIDE

A

LYDGETTS JUNCTION
AND SMELT WAGON

N

DIRECTION TIPS

A - At Lydgetts Junction turn left
before smelt wagon onto track
behind car park. Continue to minor
road and right. After about 60m go
right onto track to meet main road
and cross straight over.

B - Continue over open land towards
Consett. Follow waymarkings of yellow
background and white horseshoe
(Derwent Walk).

C - Bear right on meeting minor road to
junction with road by Rose and Crown.
Right here and in 30m left onto track
before chapel building.

| 0 | KM | 2 |

| 0 | Miles | 2 |

CONSETT - TYNEMOUTH

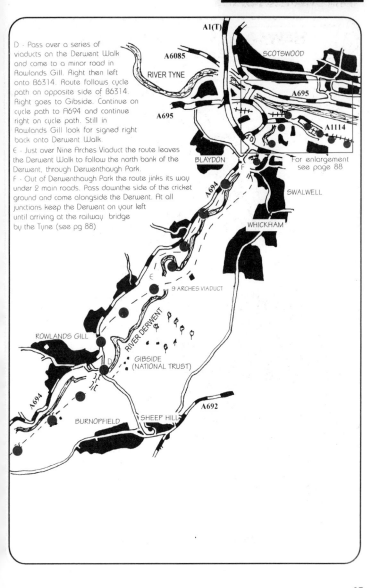

D - Pass over a series of viaducts on the Derwent Walk and come to a minor road in Rowlands Gill. Right then left onto B6314. Route follows cycle path on opposite side of B6314. Right goes to Gibside. Continue on cycle path to A694 and continue right on cycle path. Still in Rowlands Gill look for signed right back onto Derwent Walk.

E - Just over Nine Arches Viaduct the route leaves the Derwent Walk to follow the north bank of the Derwent, through Derwenthaugh Park.

F - Out of Derwenthaugh Park the route jinks its way under 2 main roads. Pass down the side of the cricket ground and come alongside the Derwent. At all junctions keep the Derwent on your left until arriving at the railway bridge by the Tyne (see pg 88)

A1(T)

A6085

SCOTSWOOD

RIVER TYNE

A695

A695

A1114

For enlargement see page 88

BLAYDON

F

SWALWELL

A694

WHICKHAM

E

9 ARCHES VIADUCT

RIVER DERWENT

ROWLANDS GILL

D

GIBSIDE (NATIONAL TRUST)

A694

BURNOPFIELD

SHEEP HILL

A692

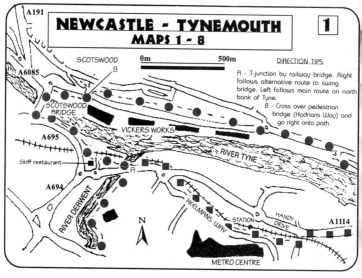

NEWCASTLE - TYNEMOUTH
MAPS 1 - 8

1

SCOTSWOOD

0m   500m

A191

A6085

SCOTSWOOD BRIDGE

VICKERS WORKS

A695

Skiff restaurant

A694

RIVER DERWENT

RIVER TYNE

KEELMANS WAY

STATION

HANDY DRIVE

A1114

N

METRO CENTRE

DIRECTION TIPS

A - T-junction by railway bridge. Right follows alternative route to swing bridge. Left follows main route on north bank of Tyne.

B - Cross over pedestrian bridge (Hadrians Way) and go right onto path.

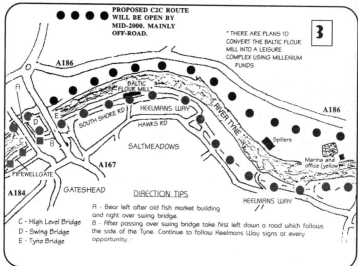

PROPOSED C2C ROUTE WILL BE OPEN BY MID-2000. MAINLY OFF-ROAD.

3

* THERE ARE PLANS TO CONVERT THE BALTIC FLOUR MILL INTO A LEISURE COMPLEX USING MILLENIUM FUNDS

A186

BALTIC FLOUR MILL *

SOUTH SHORE RD

KEELMANS WAY

HAWKS RD

SALTMEADOWS

A167

RIVER TYNE

A186

Spillers

Marina and office (yellow)

KEELMANS WAY

PIPEWELLGATE

A184   GATESHEAD

C - High Level Bridge
D - Swing Bridge
E - Tyne Bridge

DIRECTION TIPS

A - Bear left after old fish market building and right over swing bridge.

B - After passing over swing bridge take first left down a road which follows the side of the Tyne. Continue to follow Keelmans Way signs at every opportunity.

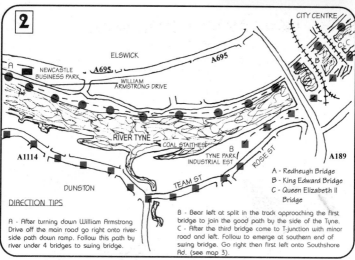

2

CITY CENTRE

ELSWICK

A695

A695

A — NEWCASTLE BUSINESS PARK

WILLIAM ARMSTRONG DRIVE

RIVER TYNE

COAL STAITHES

B

TYNE PARK INDUSTRIAL EST

ROSE ST

A1114

A189

DUNSTON

TEAM ST

DIRECTION TIPS

A — Redheugh Bridge
B — King Edward Bridge
C — Queen Elizabeth II Bridge

A — After turning down William Armstrong Drive off the main road go right onto riverside path down ramp. Follow this path by river under 4 bridges to swing bridge.

B — Bear left at split in the track approaching the first bridge to join the good path by the side of the Tyne.
C — After the third bridge come to T-junction with minor road and left. Follow to emerge at southern end of swing bridge. Go right then first left onto Southshore Rd. (see map 3).

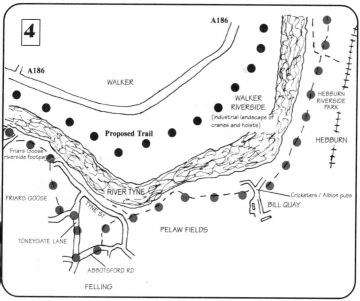

4

A186

A186

WALKER

WALKER RIVERSIDE
(industrial landscape of cranes and hoists)

HEBBURN RIVERSIDE PARK

HEBBURN

Proposed Trail

Friars Goose riverside footpath

RIVER TYNE

Cricketers / Albion pubs

FRIARS GOOSE

TYNE ST

BILL QUAY

PELAW FIELDS

TONEYGATE LANE

ABBOTSFORD RD

FELLING

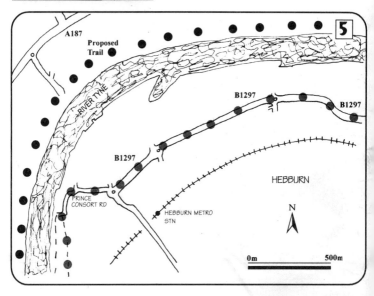

5

A187

Proposed
Trail

RIVER TYNE

B1297

B1297

B1297

HEBBURN

PRINCE
CONSORT RD

HEBBURN METRO
STN

N

0m   500m

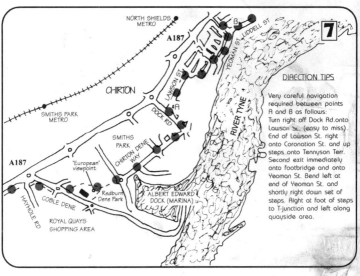

7

NORTH SHIELDS
METRO

A187

B

YEOMAN ST   LIDDELL ST

LAWSON ST

CHIRTON

A

DOCK RD

SMITHS PARK
METRO

SMITHS
PARK

RIVER TYNE

CHIRTON DENE
WAY

A187

'European'
viewpoint

Redburn
Dene Park

ALBERT EDWARD
DOCK (MARINA)

HAYHOLE RD

COBLE DENE

ROYAL QUAYS
SHOPPING AREA

DIRECTION TIPS

Very careful navigation
required between points
A and B as follows:
Turn right off Dock Rd.onto
Lawson St. (easy to miss).
End of Lawson St. right
onto Coronation St. and up
steps onto Tennyson Terr.
Second exit immediately
onto footbridge and onto
Yeoman St. Bend left at
end of Yeoman St. and
shortly right down set of
steps. Right at foot of steps
to T-junction and left along
quayside area.

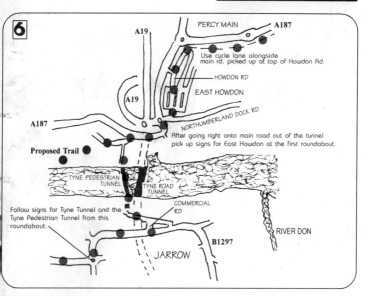

6

A19

PERCY MAIN   A187

Use cycle lane alongside main rd, picked up at top of Howdon Rd.

HOWDON RD

EAST HOWDON

A19

NORTHUMBERLAND DOCK RD

A187

After going right onto main road out of the tunnel pick up signs for East Howdon at the first roundabout.

Proposed Trail

TYNE PEDESTRIAN TUNNEL

TYNE ROAD TUNNEL

COMMERCIAL RD

Follow signs for Tyne Tunnel and the Tyne Pedestrian Tunnel from this roundabout.

RIVER DON

B1297

JARROW

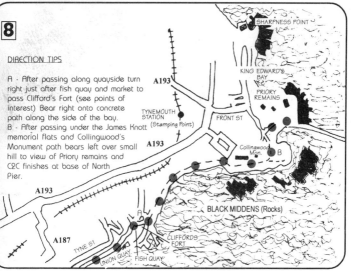

8

DIRECTION TIPS

A - After passing along quayside turn right just after fish quay and market to pass Clifford's Fort (see points of interest) Bear right onto concrete path along the side of the bay.
B - After passing under the James Knott memorial flats and Collingwood's Monument path bears left over small hill to view of Priory remains and C2C finishes at base of North Pier.

SHARPNESS POINT

KING EDWARD'S BAY

PRIORY REMAINS

A193

TYNEMOUTH STATION (Stamping Point)

FRONT ST

A193

Collingwood Mon.   B

A193

BLACK MIDDENS (Rocks)

A187

TYNE ST

CLIFFORDS FORT

UNION QUAY   FISH QUAY

91

INDEX
CITIES, TOWNS AND VILLAGES

Italic page numbers denote map entries

ACCOMMODATION INDEX

Arranged west to east along the route. The following are B&B accomodation. Campsites are indicated by the appropriate village within the main body of the text using the **Λ** sign.

ABOUT THE AUTHOR

Richard Peace is a freelance author and photographer. He was educated at Queen Elizabeth Grammar School, Wakefield and Magdalen College, Oxford. After several periods of foreign travel he qualified as a solicitor and began outdoor writing as a hobby during his time in a solicitor's office.

OTHER BOOKS BY RICHARD PEACE

Illustrated with either drawings/ photos and come complete with sketch maps and lots of other practical information.

CYCLING GUIDES

THE ULTIMATE WEST COUNTRY WAY GUIDE ISBN 1-901464-03-2
Excellent Books
Sustrans classic 250 mile route through Cornwall, Devon and Somerset. Traffic-free paths, canal towpaths and minor roads carry you to your finish in either Bristol or Bath.

YORKSHIRE DALES CYCLE WAY £5.50 ISBN 1-870141-28-8
Hillside Publications
An outstanding 130 mile route circling the entire national park and beginning in the market town of Skipton. Malham, Settle, Ingleton, Dent, Hawes and Swaledale precede a superb return down Wharfedale to Grassington.

WEST YORKSHIRE CYCLE WAY £4.99 ISBN 1-870141-38-5
Hillside Publications
This 152 mile route starts in Haworth and takes in many of the contrasts of West Yorkshire, from pastoral plains to rolling Pennine scenery Visit Otley Chevin, Pontefract Castle, Aberford and the Worth and Holme valleys

MOUNTAIN BIKING WEST AND SOUTH YORKSHIRE £5.99
ISBN 1-870141-40-7 Hillside Publications
20 day rides between 8.5 and 16.5 miles ranging from the high Pennines to the rolling plains of the east. Includes Ilkley Moor, Calderdale, Holme Valley, Barnsley Canal, Dove Valley and many more areas for hours of off-road fun.

BIKING COUNTRY GLASGOW, CLYDE VALLEY AND LOCH LOMOND £5.99
ISBN 1-870141-45-8 Hillside Publications
18 well-researched and attractive routes exploring Glasgow's hidden corners.

MOUNTAIN BIKE LANCASHIRE AND SOUTH PENNINES £5.99
ISBN 1-901464-00-8 Excellent Books
20 routes, largely off-road, visiting numerous scenic highlights in the Red Rose county and the South Pennines. From 6.5 to 20 miles to suit all levels, from beginner to experienced mountain biker. Includes famed scenery such as the Bowland Fells and Pendle Witch Country as well as other lesser known gems.

LEISURE RIDES IN THE PEAK DISTRICT AND DERBYSHIRE £5.95
ISBN 1-901464-01-6 Excellent Books
25 trails and circular routes throughout the Peak District and Derbyshire. Ideal for families and occasional or leisure riders. Many moderate length outings with longer linear outings allowing you to do as much or as little as you like. Practical advice on cycling with children plus cycle hire and eating details. Routes cover the Dark and the White Peak areas and visitor attractions such as Chatsworth.

WALKING AND GENERAL GUIDES

YORK WALKS £2.50 ISBN 1-870141-47-4 Hillside Publications
5 classic walks around the city of York exploring the major tourist sites and many lesser known features. Each theme walk traces an aspect of York's development over the centuries. Additional features include children's attractions and interesting historic inns.

THE MACLEHOSE TRAIL AND ITS SURROUNDINGS £7.99
ISBN 962-7335-14-2 The Alternative Press, Hong Kong
Written during the author's period in Hong Kong teaching English, this is a complete practical guide to the superb 100 kilometre walking trail that crosses the mountainous New Territories of Hong Kong. A superb blend of cityscape and wild countryside add up to a once-in-a-lifetime experience.

LANCASHIRE CURIOSITIES £6.95
ISBN 1-874336-42-3 The Dovecote Press
The latest in the line of the Dovecote Press's popular look at follies, buildings and all things curious on a county by county basis. 80 interesting sites county wide, profusely illustrated with quality black and white photographs.

THE ABOVE BOOKS MAY BE OBTAINED AT ALL GOOD BOOK SHOPS OR DIRECT FROM EXCELLENT BOOKS (CONTACT DETAILS AT FRONT OF BOOK).

CALLING ALL C2CERS!

Do you have any constructive comments or updates to information on the C2C route or this guide? As a dedicated and responsible publishing company we want to keep our guides as useful and bang up-to-date as possible, as we recognise that, over time, some changes may occur to route details. New editions are frequently updated and as guides are not bound until distribution to bookshops the latest information can be included in an addendum. Send in your comments and/or information updates on the route and we will send a free guide of your choice to authors of the best letters (unfortunately not every letter will get a guide). You can also keep up to date with the latest releases from Excellent Books by requesting our free catalogue. All communications should be sent to:

Excellent Books
94 Bradford Road
Wakefield
West Yorkshire
WF1 2AE
Tel / Fax: 01924 - 315147

WANT TO KNOW MORE ABOUT SUSTRANS?

Full details of other Sustrans routes and a catalogue of their route maps, other products and subscription details are available by dialing their public information line on (0117) 9290888.